FROM REVIVAL TO

TURN THE TIDE

MICHAEL L. BROWN, PhD

CHARISMA
HOUSE

TURN THE TIDE by Michael L. Brown, PhD
Published by Charisma House, an imprint of Charisma Media
1150 Greenwood Blvd., Lake Mary, Florida 32746

Copyright © 2024 by Michael L. Brown, PhD. All rights
reserved.

Unless otherwise noted, all Scripture quotations are taken
from the Holy Bible, New International Version®, NIV®.
Copyright © 1973, 1978, 1984, 2011 by Biblica, Inc.® Used by
permission of Zondervan. All rights reserved worldwide. www.
zondervan.com. The "NIV" and "New International Version"
are trademarks registered in the United States Patent and
Trademark Office by Biblica, Inc.®

Scripture quotations marked CJB are from the Complete
Jewish Bible, copyright © 1998 by David H. Stern. All rights
reserved.

Scripture quotations marked ESV are from The ESV® Bible
(The Holy Bible, English Standard Version®), copyright © 2001
by Crossway, a publishing ministry of Good News Publishers.
Used by permission. All rights reserved.

Scripture quotations marked MSG are from *The Message: The
Bible in Contemporary English*, copyright © 1993, 1994, 1995,
1996, 2000, 2001, 2002. Used by permission of NavPress
Publishing Group.

Scripture quotations marked PHILLIPS are from *The New
Testament in Modern English*, Revised Edition. Copyright ©
1958, 1960, 1972 by J. B. Phillips. Macmillan Publishing Co.
Used by permission.

Scripture quotations marked TLB are taken from *The Living
Bible*, copyright © 1971 by Tyndale House Foundation. Used
by permission of Tyndale House Publishers, Carol Stream,
Illinois 60188. All rights reserved.

While the author has made every effort to provide accurate, up-to-date source information at the time of publication, statistics and other data are constantly updated. Neither the publisher nor the author assumes any responsibility for errors or for changes that occur after publication. Further, the publisher and author do not have any control over and do not assume any responsibility for third-party websites or their content.

For more resources like this, visit MyCharismaShop.com and the author's website at askdrbrown.org.

Cataloging-in-Publication Data is on file with the Library of Congress.
International Standard Book Number: 978-1-63641-357-0
E-book ISBN: 978-1-63641-358-7

1 2024
Printed in the United States of America

Most Charisma Media products are available at special quantity discounts for bulk purchase for sales promotions, premiums, fund-raising, and educational needs. For details, call us at (407) 333-0600 or visit our website at www.charismamedia.com.

CONTENTS

PREFACE

THIS IS THE second book in the From Revival to Reformation series. The first book, *Seize the Moment: How to Fuel the Fires of Revival*, was released in January 2024, focusing on the importance of recognizing seasons of unusual divine visitation—seasons of revival—and seizing those sacred moments so as to ride these holy waves as long as possible. In the words of Leonard Ravenhill, "The opportunity of a lifetime needs to be seized during the lifetime of the opportunity."[1]

In this new book I focus on one crucial question: When revival does come, how can we move from outpouring in the church to awakening in society? Put another way, how do we move from revival to reformation?

To be sure, the principles outlined in this book are always relevant for God's people as we seek to function as the salt of the earth and the light of the world. How with the Spirit's help can we be agents of positive change? What can we do to stand for justice and transformation? Using the weapons of prayer and the gospel, how can we advance God's kingdom on the earth until Jesus returns?

Yet we cannot give what we do not have, and if the church is unhealthy, we cannot make the world any healthier. If our light is deficient, we cannot brighten the world. As Jesus said, "You are the salt of the earth. But if the salt loses its saltiness, how can it be made salty again? It is no longer good for anything, except to be thrown out and trampled underfoot" (Matt. 5:13). And in a slightly different context, "If then the light within you is darkness, how great is that darkness!" (Matt. 6:23). As I have said for many years, my greatest concern is not so much the presence of darkness in America as it is the absence of light.

This book, then, focuses on the light—meaning on us—helping us realize how we can see genuine, lasting social transformation by implementing the principles laid out for us in Scripture and fleshed out over the centuries. But to repeat, we can do this only if we ourselves are healthy. Conversely, a true revival movement, as powerful and lasting as its effects can be, is not guaranteed to bring about societal change—hence this two-book series, with each book standing completely on its own.

Over twenty-five years ago the Spirit began to speak to me that as surely as there was a Civil Rights Movement in America, there will be a gospel-based moral and cultural revolution in America. In recent years we have seen increasing evidence that this revolution is underway, as more and more Americans are saying "Enough!" to today's cultural madness. But this revolutionary movement will succeed only if believers lead the way, and that's what this book is about. May the Lord give us ears to hear and a heart to respond. Every single one of us has an important role to play.

My thanks once again to the entire Charisma Media team for embracing the vision of these books and helping to get them published in a timely fashion, to my own team at The Line of Fire, and to those who have hungered and thirsted for Jesus to be glorified in this hour and are ready to seize the moment and turn the tide. On with it!

—Michael L. Brown
January 31, 2024

PART I

SETTING THE STAGE

PART I

SETTING THE STAGE

CHAPTER 1

A SOBER WARNING: WE DARE NOT SQUANDER THIS MOMENT

W E ARE LIVING at a critical moment in American history. How we respond today will go a long way in determining the future of our nation— or whether our nation even continues to exist as the United States of America. That's why the title of my October 2021 book was *Revival or We Die: A Great Awakening Is Our Only Hope.*[1] There was no hyperbole in the title and no exaggeration in the subtitle. I believed then and believe now that without a sweeping revival in the church that leads to a national awakening, America as we know it is doomed. We will either continue to fall into moral and spiritual confusion, ultimately crashing and burning, or we will break up entirely as a nation, pulling apart at the seams. Either way, without revival we are in very critical condition.

But here's the catch. Revival alone will not get the job done. Revival alone will not turn the tide. It must be a revival in the church that leads to a reformation in society, an outpouring that leads to awakening. Otherwise, to repeat, we are doomed. A powerful revival movement without a national awakening would just delay the inevitable or, worse still, simply make us more accountable. It really is revival and awakening, or we die. Or do we really think that the right political candidate or the latest social program will solve our problems and cure our ills? Not a chance.

How do we fix things when most American adolescents are "viewing online pornographic videos with motions and sounds, depicting every potential sexual act that can be imagined,"[2] and when "the majority of kids are exposed to porn by age 13, with some exposed as young as seven, according to a 2020 survey"?[3] How do we fix *that*?

How do we fix things when 40 percent of our children are born out of wedlock,[4] with half of all births to first-time mothers occurring out of wedlock?[5] As far back as 2013, "eighty-three percent of first births to non-high school graduates [were] to unwed mothers," and "by 30, two-thirds of women will have had a child out of wedlock."[6] As of 2019, America had the "world's highest rate of children living in single-parent households."[7] What is the political or social solution to problems like this?

How do we fix things when Americans with no religious affiliation rose from almost 0 percent in the 1950s to almost one-fifth of the US adult population by 2021?[8] In 2011, 75 percent of Americans identified as Christian. By 2021, that number had dropped to 63 percent, the most rapid drop in recorded polling history.[9] How do we right the ship?

How do we fix things when there have been 389 school shootings since Columbine,[10] some of them more deadly than that tragic event?[11] How do we fix things when every day we become more deeply and dangerously divided over important issues such as abortion, transgender rights, and free speech? What is the earthly solution?

Take something as simple (and apparently minor) as shoplifting. Even that has reached epidemic levels. As reported by David Marcus in the *Daily Mail*,

There is anarchy in the USA.

More and more, Americans are living every day in a dystopia that just a few years ago would have been utterly unimaginable.

From major cities to the border, and even in some suburbs, the rule of law is now all but meaningless, with hard-working families left to pay the price in blood and treasure.

The America we grew up in—of bright shopping malls that weren't attacked by thieving mobs, of gas stations where carjacking wasn't commonplace, and of public transport that didn't double as a homeless shelter—is vanishing.

Last week came the sobering figure that our country now has [a] $100 billion-a-year shoplifting habit.

One hundred billion dollars. The annual budget for the entire state of Maryland is a mere $65 billion.

And this is money that, according to the National Retail Federation, stores are never getting back. As brazen crooks stuff backpacks full of goods unchallenged, the police—cripplingly over-stretched—will likely never even turn up.[12]

How do we fix all this or even begin to chip away at these problems short of a sweeping spiritual revival that will produce a moral and cultural revolution? There is no other way to turn the tide.

THE HOUR IS MORE URGENT THAN WE REALIZE

Speaking to a group of Catholic priests around the year 2010, Cardinal Francis George (1937–2015) said, "I expect to die in bed, my successor will die in prison and his successor will die a martyr in the public square. His successor will pick up the shards of a ruined society and slowly help rebuild civilization, as the church has done so often in human history."[13] What profound words!

Cardinal George subsequently explained that he was responding to a question when he gave this spontaneous answer, which was "entirely outside of the current political debate." And he noted that he "was trying to express in overly dramatic fashion what the complete secularization of our society could bring." He certainly hit the nail on the head.

In my view, speaking as soberly as I can, the picture that Cardinal George painted is entirely plausible, barring one thing and only one thing: a sweeping revival that produces a radical reformation to our society, a spiritual renewal so deep it births a societal awakening. Otherwise, the crash is inevitable. (Of course, if Jesus returns in the next few years, this point will be moot.)

Some may protest that we've been here many times before in our history, with doomsayers repeatedly claiming that the end of the world was near. "It's all over," they shouted in years past. "America is doomed!" And yet here we are today, decades (or centuries) later, still economically strong, still powerful, still one nation. Perhaps I'm overstating things.

I've written extensively on this very subject, giving examples of times past when it appeared that it was all over for America (or at least for the church of America).[14] Yet the tide turned, God poured out His Spirit, and America marched on. Obviously, the doomsday prophets were wrong. Perhaps my concerns will prove empty too.

But here is the threefold, jarring reality: 1) It was powerful revival movements in the past that turned the tide and saved the nation. Nothing less will do so today. 2) In many ways, we have been on a steady moral and spiritual decline since the counterculture revolution of the 1960s. So it really is revival or we die. 3) There is no guarantee that America will not go the way of the Roman Empire, fading into oblivion, or have a fate similar to the USSR, breaking into fragments. (The Soviet Union dissolved into fifteen independent states.)[15] Show me where it is written that this will not happen to our country. Show me the chapter and verse.

After all, if the covenant nation, Israel, could suffer dispersal, exile, and near complete destruction, continuing to exist as a people only because of the sovereign mercy of God, why should we assume that America's blessed destiny is guaranteed? Again, I tell you: show me the chapter and verse.

Speaking at the commencement exercises at Harvard University in 1978, the famed Russian novelist Aleksandr Solzhenitsyn brought a sobering word to the graduating class. Describing the horrors of the Communist Revolution, he said, "If I were asked today to formulate as concisely as possible what was the main cause of the ruinous revolution that swallowed up some 60 million of our people, I could not put it more accurately than to repeat: 'Men had forgotten God; that is why all this has happened.'"

Speaking of America, he said this:

> There are telltale symptoms by which history gives warning to a threatened or perishing society. Such are, for instance, a decline of the arts or a lack of great statesmen. Indeed, sometimes the warnings are quite explicit and concrete. The center of your democracy and of your culture is left without electric power

for a few hours only, and all of a sudden crowds of American citizens start looting and creating havoc. The smooth surface film must be very thin, then, the social system quite unstable and unhealthy.

And he uttered these words back in 1978. I shudder to think what he would say if he were alive today. We are, in so many ways, a nation that has forgotten God. To quote once more from this historic speech: "To destroy a people, you must first sever their roots."[16] Could Solzhenitsyn have been any clearer?

Writing eight years earlier, in 1970, Christian philosopher Francis Schaeffer spoke plainly of America as a post-Christian nation. Elliot Clark summarized it.

> He writes about the reality of historic Christianity becoming the minority in the West, stripped of cultural power and influence. And in this situation, Schaeffer identifies a great danger for evangelicals: taking sides with political elites in order to retain comfort, affluence, and personal peace. In the face of societal chaos and upheaval, Schaeffer doesn't want Christians to compromise for the sake of short-lived comfort.
>
> In this remarkably prescient work, Schaeffer goes on to predict the inevitable loss of freedoms that will come once the Christian foundations of Western society have finally crumbled. And in response, Schaeffer calls for a kind of culture war—though not the sort of battles we might be imagining. Schaeffer wants a Christian revolution, the kind that looks like spiritual reformation.[17]

Yet even a Christian thinker as brilliant as Schaeffer might struggle to find the right words to describe the current state of our nation, one in which thirteen-year-old girls are encouraged by doctors to have their healthy breasts removed simply because they are temporarily confused about their gender identity;[18] one in which men's bathrooms on college campuses have tampons, since "men can menstruate" too;[19] one in which you can be banned from social media for "deadnaming" or "misgendering" someone (for example, calling Caitlyn Jenner "Bruce" or referring to him as "he"); one in which music videos saturated with the most profane, graphic, and degrading sexual imagery are watched or downloaded hundreds of millions of times;[20] one in which fentanyl overdoses have become the leading cause of death for adults between eighteen and forty-five;[21] one in which a Christian pastor who made reference to homosexual practice in a sermon fifteen years earlier was disinvited from praying at a presidential inauguration while a gay bishop was invited to offer up special prayers by this same president four years earlier;[22] one in which a major sports team publicly honored an anti-Catholic, Jesus-mocking drag group called the Sisters of Perpetual Indulgence;[23] one in which we now have more millennial witches than Presbyterians.[24] Need I say more?

Journalist and cultural commentator Christopher Rufo said,

> The cultural revolution that began a half-century ago, now reflected in a deadening sequence of acronyms—CRT, DEI, ESG, and more—has increasingly become our new official morality. Many conservatives have made an uneasy peace with this

transformation of values, even as the culture around them has, in many places, collapsed.

This attitude no longer suffices. It is time to break the loop of 1968. We need a counterrevolution.[25]

He is absolutely right, but I would take this one step further. This counterrevolution must be gospel based. That's why our only hope is a sweeping national revival that turns into a powerful cultural awakening. It is the purpose of this book to lay out just how this can be done, all by the empowerment, grace, and guidance of the Lord.

CHAPTER 2

FROM OUTPOURING TO AWAKENING: THE NEED FOR STRATEGIC THINKING

I N THE MIDST of a powerful outpouring of the Spirit, it feels as if all your dreams have come true. You are experiencing what you have longed for and prayed for, and the Lord Himself is so near. Lives are being dramatically changed, the crowds keep pouring in, and the worship is powerful. This is it! Revival is here! At last! For good reason, you are grateful beyond words. The Lord has answered your prayers. The Lord has seen your tears. The Lord has heard your cries.

But how would you feel ten or twenty or thirty years later if there was little or nothing to show for the revival, no lasting fruit from the outpouring? How would you feel if most of the converts had fallen back into their old ways, if very few new churches and ministries had been birthed, if there was no lasting effect on your community, if your own congregation had not grown and deepened, if all that remained were stories of the revival? How would you feel then?

Certainly, in the midst of a genuine revival, it seems as if long-term results are virtually guaranteed. After all, the Spirit is moving so deeply and people are being changed so radically that substantial, lasting fruit seems like a given. And in some ways it *is* a given, since many of those who were powerfully touched during real seasons of revival *are* changed for life. You can count on it. That is the very nature of revival.

On the other hand, without intentionality and long-term vision, it is very possible that much of the fruit of the revival will be short-lived. The fires will die out, the passion will wane, the enthusiasm will dissipate, and the consecration will erode. Those who became hot will turn lukewarm (or even cold) again. Those who became radical will become ordinary. Those who talked about changing the world will become like the world. How tragic that would be!

The bad news is that in too many instances the lasting fruit of a season of revival is much less than it could have been. The good news is that this does not have to be the case with the current (or next) wave of revival, since God's will is that revival results in long-term, glorious, world-impacting fruit. Church history is replete with many wonderful, Jesus-exalting examples.

In *The Revival Answer Book*, I shared that John Wesley (1703–1791), the founder of the Methodist movement, was vilified by many clergymen, including a vocal opponent named Rev. John Kirkby.

> Writing in 1750, twelve years after Wesley's famous conversion, Rev. John Kirkby described "the horrid blasphemies and impieties taught by those dia-bolical seducers called Methodists." He continued: "They pray in the language of a saint to Beelzebub himself," and "their religion could be forged nowhere but in the bottomless pit." And how did he speak of Wesley himself, one of the saintliest men

ever to grace the Church? Kirkby called him "that emissary of Satan," whose religion is "as opposite to Christianity as heaven is to hell", and "whose damnation will be just." (Remember: This was written by a concerned minister!)[1]

But that is hardly the end of the story. I noted that

the verdict of history has been radically different. The prominent French historian, Professor Elie Halévy, claimed that "it would be *difficult to overestimate* the part played by the Wesleyan revival" in transforming England, actually calling it "the moral cement" of the society and stating that the revival explained "the miracle of modern England." In 1928, Archbishop Davidson observed that it was "not too much to say that Wesley practically changed the outlook and even the character of the English nation," while in 1922, British Prime Minister Lloyd George said that the Wesleyan movement was responsible for "a complete revolution effected in the whole country" of Wales, and that it was impossible to explain *nineteenth* century England without first explaining Wesley. In fact, he claimed that "you cannot understand *twentieth* century America, unless you understand Wesley." And this was the man who was sometimes pelted with rocks and feces when he preached![2]

SOME EXAMPLES OF LASTING FRUIT

Back in the 1990s, my wife Nancy's father bought our family a subscription to *Reader's Digest*. We had never expressed interest in the publication, but it was enjoyable to receive and often had some interesting quotes or articles. One day Nancy said to me, "You need to read this article," telling me about a story in the July 1994 issue of the magazine. But I forgot she had mentioned it to me, failing to look at it at all. Not long after that, while preaching on revival for a pastor in Poway, California, he pointed me to an amazing *Reader's Digest* article written by John S. Tompkins titled "Our Kindest City." I was stirred as I read it, sharing my enthusiasm with Nancy. She replied to me, "That's the article I told you to read!" (Yes, fellow husbands, I get it. We need to listen better when our wives give us advice.)

What then was so important about this article, especially when it came to the subject of revival? Tompkins, a journalist, not a minister, had wondered why it was that the city of Rochester, New York, was rated the kindest, most altruistic city in the nation in two separate polls, one taken in 1940, and the other in 1990–92. He discovered the surprising answer. In 1830 he wrote Charles Finney (1792–1875)

> spent six months in Rochester and converted hundreds of residents—lawyers, doctors, judges, tradesmen, bankers, boatmen, workers, master craftsmen—to born-again Christianity. He scorched their consciences and urged them not to follow the selfish ways of the world. Finney angrily denounced the evils of selfishness and deliberately aimed his message at the wealthy and powerful....
>
> Having converted the affluent, Finney's final step was to get them to direct their energy and wealth into beneficial philanthropies. He was amazingly successful. Rochester embarked on a church-building

boom. Rochesterians went on to establish a university, organize charities and self-help agencies, build a public-school system, fight against slavery (the city was a station on the Underground Railroad, which smuggled slaves into Canada), form unions and reform the prison system. Rochester became a city where love for one's fellow man was more than an empty phrase.[3]

By 2019 a Barna survey placed Rochester as the eighth-most post-Christian city in America, indicating that nothing in this world lasts forever. But the thought of a six-month revival in 1829–1830 still bearing fruit more than 160 years later is absolutely mind-boggling. Many of us would be thrilled with fruit that lasted a decade, let alone a generation. But fruit that lasted more than a century and a half? How incredible is that!

During the Brownsville Revival (1995–2000), all of us in leadership wanted to see fruit that would last. That's one reason we raised up a school of ministry, which in turn birthed a missions organization to cover and support the graduates. Today, as I write these words roughly twenty-eight years after the revival began, I can point you to significant Christian works taking place around the world that are a direct result of the revival, ones with which I am personally familiar. I'm talking about ministries that are feeding the hungry, caring for orphans, rescuing victims of human trafficking, educating impoverished children, and reaching Muslims and Hindus, with these ministry leaders now sending their spiritual (and even natural) sons and daughters into the mission field. (For a sampling, see the missionaries listed on our Fire International website, fire-international.org, most of whom are our graduates. But note that we cannot list the activities, identities, and locations of those working in some persecuted nations.)

I can point you to ministry school grads who are doing amazing things for the Lord in prominent national and international settings. I can also point you to grads whose names are not well known but who have married and then raised godly children with high morals and strong spirituality, and they are doing this because they were deeply touched in the revival. I can also point you to a stream of converts of the revival who love Jesus to this day.[4] This is lasting fruit.

Some of this came about as the virtually automatic result of the revival, since the conversions and transformations were so profound, while some of this is the result of careful and prayerful planning and action, all with the very specific goal of bearing lasting fruit. (My previous book, *Seize the Moment: How to Fuel the Fires of Revival*, published in January 2024, is also relevant in this regard.)

At the same time, I cannot point to the lasting impact of the revival on the *city* of Pensacola, although at the height of the revival the whole city knew what was taking place, and the superintendent of schools for the county told me about the powerful effect the revival had had on the local schools as early as October 1997. In my opinion, the revival did not have its full potential impact on the city, because after a short time it became a national and international hotspot, with as many as three million people coming to Pensacola (cumulatively) from more than 130 nations. So while the impact of the revival was worldwide, the church and the leaders were not able to devote as much attention to the local community. Otherwise, I believe we could have seen a more dramatic and lasting local impact.

These are some of the challenges that come with a real move of the Spirit, all boiling down to this: What can be done to ensure long-lasting fruit? How can the move of God we are experiencing *today* be felt *tomorrow*?

The fact is that as surely as revivals come, revivals go, since it is humanly impossible to sustain the intensity of a real revival over a period of many years. Not only so, but God's goal for His people is to maintain a steady walk over the decades, to live as disciples in the grind of everyday life, to be like the Word-loving person described in Psalm 1:3, who is "like a tree planted by streams of water, which yields its fruit in season and whose leaf does not wither—whatever they do prospers." Put another way, within the church the goal is to go from visitation to habitation and from a short-term revival experience to a long-term revival culture. Outside the church the goal is to go from outpouring to awakening, from God's people being changed to the world being changed. A true revival, be it in its local or national or international expression, should make a generational impact. But how? That's the big question we intend to answer in the pages that follow.

First we need to take a few more minutes to set the stage, looking back through our recent history so we can effectively look ahead.

CHAPTER 3

CULTURAL CHANGE DOES
NOT HAPPEN BY ACCIDENT

I N 2004 LESS than four in ten Americans supported same-sex marriage, and when Senator Barack Obama campaigned for president in 2008, he felt it necessary to affirm marriage as the union of one man and one woman. If he didn't express this conviction, it was unlikely he would be elected. By the time he ran for reelection in 2012, he felt free to express his real views, namely that two men or two women could marry.[1] Not surprisingly, in 2019, four years after the Supreme Court ruled to redefine marriage, more than six in ten Americans supported same-sex marriage. Not only so, but 36 percent felt that the legalizing of these unions had had a very positive impact on society.[2] Yet in 2003, the year the Supreme Court issued its *Lawrence v. Texas* decision, the act of sodomy was technically illegal in much of the nation.

Just one generation earlier, in the 1960s, "gay men and women in New York City could not be served alcohol in public due to liquor laws that considered the gathering of homosexuals to be 'disorderly.'" And so, "In fear of being shut down by authorities, bartenders would deny drinks to patrons suspected of being gay or kick them out altogether; others would serve them drinks but force them to sit facing away from other customers to prevent them from socializing."[3] This was *in the 1960s*, even in cities such as New York. How did we get from then, a time when gays were denigrated and marginalized, to now, a time when they are celebrated and emulated?

Before the Stonewall Riots in New York City in 1969, you could be arrested simply for cross-dressing (dressing in drag),[4] while in 1994, twenty-five years after Stonewall, drag queens (along with "leathermen") were barred from New York's annual gay pride parade. They were considered more of an embarrassment than an asset.[5] Today, drag queens are celebrated on a national level to the point that the American Library Association enthusiastically supports Drag Queen Story Hour,[6] where drag queens read stories to toddlers and little children, even swinging their hips as they chant, "The hips on the drag queen go swish, swish, swish."[7] Again I ask, How on earth did such a dramatic shift take place in our culture, much of it accelerating rapidly in the last few years?

Not that long ago Americans would have scoffed at the idea of Bruce Jenner becoming Caitlyn Jenner, let alone his being named *Glamour* magazine's Woman of the Year (he received this award in 2015). It would have sounded more like satire than reality, just as the idea of "menstruating men" would have struck us as some kind of bizarre joke.[8] In the same way, we would have been absolutely shocked to hear college students explain that you are whoever and whatever you perceive yourself to be—including your gender, your ethnicity, your age, or even your *species*.[9]

We would have been mortified to think that boys who identify as girls could compete against girls in sports, let alone share bathrooms and locker rooms with them. And we would have been absolutely appalled to learn that doctors were putting ten-year-old boys and girls on irreversible, life-altering, potentially sterilizing hormone blockers to stop the onset of puberty based entirely on these children's personal perceptions and feelings. Without a doubt, most of us would have called for the criminal prosecution of such doctors, with cries of "Medical malpractice!" and "Child abuse!" erupting throughout the land.

Yet in 2020, candidate Joe Biden made transgender rights a pillar of his presidential platform, fighting aggressively for the "rights" of boys to compete in sports against girls (and share their personal and private spaces) and for the "rights" of doctors to chemically castrate and genetically mutilate children.[10] And in 2023, Fox News, the most prominent conservative voice on cable TV, hired Bruce "Caitlyn" Jenner as a consultant and regular guest.[11]

How is all this possible? How did such radical, even shocking, changes come about? I can assure you that none of this happened accidentally.

In 2011, when my book *A Queer Thing Happened to America* was published (we had to self-publish the book because no major publisher, secular or Christian, was willing to touch it), the idea of a "gay agenda" was widely ridiculed by LGBTQ+ activists, let alone by your average LGBT-identified person. That's one reason the book was so meticulously documented (seven hundred pages long with roughly fifteen hundred endnotes), with the first chapter titled "A Stealth Agenda." In it I examined the question of whether a gay (or LGBT) agenda actually existed.

After citing a long list of gay denials that such an agenda did exist, I supplied quote after quote and example after example that proved the exact opposite, closing the chapter with these words:

> In the last four decades, major changes have taken place in: 1) the public's perception of homosexuality and same-sex relationships; 2) the educational system's embrace of homosexuality; 3) legislative decisions recognizing gays and lesbians as a distinct group of people within our society, equivalent to other ethnic groups; 4) the media's portrayal of LGBT people; and 5) corporate America's welcoming of what was once considered unacceptable behavior. Is this simply one big coincidence? Did all this happen by chance? Don't these very results—which barely tell the story—give evidence to a clearly defined gay agenda?

Well, just in case you're not 100% sure, a leading gay activist has helped remove all doubt. Speaking shortly after the 2006 elections, Matt Foreman, then the executive director of the National Gay and Lesbian Task Force, had this to say:

> "You want to know the state of our movement on November 10, 2006? We are strong, unbowed, unbeaten, vibrant, energized and ready to kick some butt."

And what exactly does this mean?

"The agenda and vision that we must proudly articulate is that yes, indeed, we intend to change society."[12]

Or, in the words of gay leader (and former seminary professor) Dr. Mel White,

> It is time for a campaign of relentless non-violent resistance that will convince our adversaries to do justice at last. They have

assumed that we are infinitely patient or
too comfortable to call for revolution. For
their sake, and for the sake of the nation,
we must prove them wrong.

So, the cat is out of the bag and the covert agenda is
becoming overt, backed by a movement that proclaims
itself "strong, unbowed, unbeaten, vibrant, energized
and ready to kick some butt." It is nothing less than a
gay revolution—and it is coming to a school or court
or business or house of worship near you.
America, are you ready?[13]

Sadly, in retrospect, the answer to this final question is
a resounding no. America was not ready, and the results
have been tragic.

But there is good news in the midst of this rapid
social and moral decline. Not only are many Christians
pushing back against this unhealthy agenda, but many
non-religious, mainstream Americans are pushing back
too. (I'll focus on this in chapter 4, but let me emphasize here that when I say "pushing back," I do not mean
hating or demeaning those who identify as LGBTQ+, nor
do I mean depriving them of equal rights under the law.
I mean resisting their activist goals.) I have been documenting this pushback for years, and the relevant articles
I have written during this time could easily fill several
books. Real progress is being made. (On a broader level,
the overturning of *Roe v. Wade* in 2022 was of momentous importance.)

But this is also a teachable moment, one in which we
need to ask ourselves how, exactly, LGBTQ+ activists, with
the help of their straight allies, were able to bring about such

dramatic changes in such a short period of time. What were some of the keys to the LGBTQ+ revolution? How is it that Linda Hirshman, herself a heterosexual, could write a book in 2012 titled *Victory: The Triumphant Gay Revolution: How a Despised Minority Pushed Back, Beat Death, Found Love, and Changed America for Everyone*?[14] Not that long ago, Hollywood actors and media personalities hid their homosexual orientations, not wanting to destroy their careers. By 2012 Hirshman could note that "so many people in show business have come out as gay that some gay media are now pooh-poohing their confessions as cheap shots meant to *bolster* their flagging careers."[15]

Hirshman writes,

> In 1969, "homosexuals," people who wanted to have sex with members of their own sex, were considered sinful by the church, their sexual practices were criminal in forty-nine states, the psychiatrists said they were crazy, and the State Department held that they were subversive. Forty-two years later, almost to the day, Andrew Cuomo, the governor of the state of New York, signed the law that enabled them to marry in New York. The Empire State Building was lit up in the rainbow colors of the symbolic gay flag.[16]

Again, how did such sweeping changes take place so quickly? How did such a tiny minority of the population bring about such dramatic changes in just a few decades?

WHAT THE CHURCH CAN LEARN FROM THE LGBTQ+ REVOLUTION

In October 2007 I delivered a series of lectures on the subject of "Homosexuality, the Church, and Society." The lectures were held at the Booth Playhouse in the Blumenthal Performing Arts Center in the heart of Charlotte, North Carolina, and they attracted considerable attention from the local media. (I had no idea when we booked the venue that years earlier, in 1996, the venue came under fire for hosting a controversial play "exploring social and political themes dealing with homosexuality."[17] Locals told me the playhouse had been nicknamed "gay central.")

We announced in our advertising that we would have an open mic for a Q&A after every lecture, also stating plainly that no hate speech or gay bashing would be allowed. Our goal was to speak the truth in love and provide a forum for healthy interaction without vitriol, one in which everyone would feel safe. One of the lectures was titled "What the Church Can Learn From the Gay and Lesbian Community," and in the ninety-minute talk I made these eight points:

1. Change did not come about merely by going to gay meetings but rather by being gay 24/7. It was the same thing with civil rights. Change did not come about merely by people going to civil rights meetings but rather by joining the Civil Rights Movement! And so sooner or laterAmerican Christians will have to learn that our emphasis must be on *being* the church more than on merely *going* to church. We must get out of the audience mentality and become part of a functioning body.[18]

2. Even a tiny minority with determination and vision can change the world. Trusting in numbers and political power has always been a trap for the church, since we take our eyes off the cross—which speaks of sacrifice and service and humility—and put our faith in the power of human might. Fidel Castro said: "I began the revolution with 82 men. If I had [to] do it again, I'd do it with 10 or 15 and absolute faith. It does not matter how small you are if you have faith and a plan of action."[19] In the words of Edmund Burke, "Nobody made a greater mistake than he who did nothing because he could do only a little."[20]

3. You must come out boldly. Gay activist Marc Rubin looked back at Stonewall thirty years later and asked, "How did that singular event in June 1969 become the fountainhead for so many of the changes that have made the world so different for queers thirty years later? It spawned the Gay Liberation Movement."[21]

He added, "First there was The Gay Liberation Front proclaiming loudly, clearly, and brilliantly, the truth that gay is good, that queers had embodied within them all of the genius of humanity, and owned all privileges of that status....And so, gay shame was replaced by gay pride—in the public square, and quite boldly."[22]

How bold was boldly? Rubin wrote, "The means to achieving these ends included, street actions famously defined as "zaps", marches, picket lines, political lobbying, education, active promotion of the need for lesbians and gay men to come out of their closets, and a constant in-your-face presentation of the fact that gay is good. Its goals were revolutionary in that it sought, through these means, to restructure society."[23] And restructure society it did.

How much more, then, should we, the redeemed, blood-washed followers of Jesus, be unashamed! Jesus said:

You are the light of the world. A town built on a hill cannot be hidden. Neither do people light a lamp and put it under a bowl. Instead they put it on its stand, and it gives light to everyone in the house. In the same way, let your light shine before others, that they may see your good deeds and glorify your Father in heaven.

—MATTHEW 5:14–16

If anyone is ashamed of me and my words in this adulterous and sinful generation, the Son of Man will be ashamed of them when he comes in his Father's glory with the holy angels.

—MARK 8:38

Paul wrote:

I am not ashamed of the gospel, because it is the power of God that brings salvation to everyone who believes: first to the Jew, then for the Gentile.

—ROMANS 1:16

And he wrote this to Timothy:

So do not be ashamed of the testimony about our Lord or of me his prisoner. Rather, join with me in suffering for the gospel, by the power of God.

—2 TIMOTHY 1:8

Peter wrote:

If you suffer as a Christian, do not be ashamed, but praise God that you bear that name.

—1 PETER 4:16

We, of all people, should be bold and unashamed—and it begins with the leadership. The early gay activists risked life and limb for their cause, knowing that coming out could cost them everything. Yet all too many of us who claim to have eternal life and an intimate relationship with God aren't willing to risk personal insult or loss of income or family rejection or denomination pressure for our convictions and faith. How can this be?

4. You must focus on changing the world, not escaping from it.

Again, read what Marc Rubin said. This was the gay agenda in 1969:

- GLF, the Gay Liberation Front, was conceived as being part of the entire Liberation movement, one segment of a worldwide struggle against oppression....

- The Gay Activists Alliance stood for writing the revolution into law. Although individual members would ally themselves to causes not directly related to the oppression of homosexuals, the organization's single-issue focus enabled it to direct all of its energies toward working intensively in, on, with, and against "The Establishment" on issues effecting [sic] lesbians and gay men.

- These were the clear goals: "We demand our Liberation *from* repression and *to* the point where repressive laws are removed from the books and our rights are written into the documents that protect the rights of all people, for without that writing there can be no guarantees of protection from the larger society."[24]

And while gay activists were launching their revolution—and getting it written into law—a broad, counterculture revolution was impacting our society. Yet at the same time, many Christians were expecting Jesus to come at any moment and get them out of this world, basically handing society over to those who opposed their values.[25]

One group fought for change; the other group looked for escape. Who succeeded? We're still here, still talking about the end of the world, while others have succeeded in changing the world. Retreat always spells defeat!

Jesus gave us a battle plan. Are we following it? "All authority in heaven and on earth has been given to me. Therefore go and make disciples of all nations, baptizing them in the name of the Father and of the Son and of the Holy Spirit, and teaching them to obey everything I have commanded you. And surely I am with you always, to the very end of the age" (Matt 28:18–20).

5. Revolutions require strategy, including winning the battle of words and ideas. No one understood this better than Marshall Kirk and Hunter Madsen. Their best-selling 1989 book *After the Ball: How America Will Conquer Its Fear and Hatred of Gays in the 90's*, built on a shorter article titled "The Overhauling of Straight America." The article outlined a sixfold strategy.

1. Talk about gays and gayness as loudly and often as possible.

2. Portray gays as victims, not aggressive challengers.

3. Give [homosexual] protectors a just cause.

4. Make gays look good.

5. Make the victimizers look bad.

6. Solicit funds: the buck stops here (i.e., get corporate America and major foundations to support the homosexual cause financially).[26]

All this has happened brilliantly and dramatically, to the point that it's hard to conceive that these were actually *goals to be realized* in the late 1980s. But this was their stated purpose: the "conversion of the average American's emotions, mind, and will, through a planned psychological attack, in the form of propaganda fed to the nation via the media."[27]

Jesus said that the children of this world are shrewder in dealing with the world around them than are the children of the light (Luke 16:8). What is our strategy?[28]

6. Remember to focus on the children. This is almost a mantra in gay activist circles: The children are being hurt. Consider how this affects the children. Always talk about the children!

In his TV appearances, John Amaechi, the former NBA player who became a poster boy for the Human Rights Campaign, the world's largest gay activist organization, made constant references to young people. Organizations such as GLSEN—the Gay, Lesbian, & Straight Education Network—have targeted children, beginning with elementary school.

Need I say more to followers of Jesus today? Either we speak up for the children and make their solid upbringing and education a priority, or someone else will. Are we going to sit idly by and let our kids become victims?

7. Remember to reach out to the marginalized. This lies at the heart of gay activism, which began with a G, then quickly redefined itself as GL, and then GLBTQ and beyond (gay, lesbian, bisexual, transgender, queer/questioning, and sometimes I for intersexed and P for pansexual or pomosexual). Just look at how this list has grown since 2007!

Gays and lesbians, who were so stigmatized by society, found a home in the LGBTQ+ community, experiencing acceptance and affirmation. They were no longer outcasts. As the body of Christ, we cannot affirm homosexuality in any way, but we *must* reach out to the marginalized, to the stigmatized, to the outcasts, and to the outsiders. Jesus especially cares for them. He taught:

> Suppose one of you has a hundred sheep and loses one of them. Doesn't he leave the ninety-nine in the open country and go after the lost sheep until he finds it? And when he finds it, he joyfully puts it on his shoulders and goes home. Then he calls his friends and neighbors together and says, "Rejoice with me; I have found my lost sheep." I tell you that in the same way there will be more rejoicing in heaven over one sinner who repents than over ninety-nine righteous persons who do not need to repent.
>
> —LUKE 15:4–7

He also said:

> When you give a luncheon or dinner, do not invite your friends, your brothers or sisters, your relatives, or your rich neighbors; if you do, they may invite you back and so you will be repaid. But when you give a banquet, invite the poor, the crippled, the lame, the blind, and you will be blessed. Although

they cannot repay you, you will be repaid at the resurrection of the righteous.

—LUKE 14:12–14

I am not implying that gays and lesbians are poor, crip-
pled, lame, and blind—in fact, today they are often leaders
in many aspects of society—but I am saying that we can
apply Jesus' words to reaching out to the very people who
make us uncomfortable. I repeat: He died for them just as
He died for you and me.

8. Unity is essential. Although in some ways the homosexual community is as diverse as the heterosexual community, in other ways there is remarkable unity, solidarity,
and ability to mobilize for action within the gay community. (Christian friends of mine who attended the annual
HRC North Carolina Dinner in 2007 to observe how they
operated told me they had never seen such an energized,
unified crowd in their lives, and it included many movers
and shakers of the city.)

Yet the church is often famous for its disunity and splits.
Could it be that we are fighting for our own little kingdoms while gays and lesbians are fighting for a common
cause—as they would state it, simply the right to be
accepted as fellow human beings with equal status and
privilege as those that are afforded to heterosexuals? The
New Testament clearly calls us to unity. Jesus taught it,
prayed for it, and died for it, and the other New Testament
authors echo this call. Without unity, we are doomed to
fail.

To quote these words from the Lord, "every kingdom
divided against itself will be ruined, and every city or
household divided against itself will not stand. If Satan

drives out Satan, he is divided against himself. How then can his kingdom stand?" (Matt 12:25-26).

And note His prayer:

> My prayer is not for [the apostles] alone. I pray also for those who will believe in me through their message, that all of them may be one, Father, just as you are in me and I am in you. May they also be in us so that the world may believe that you have sent me. I have given them the glory that you gave me, that they may be one as we are one—I in them and you in me—so that they may be brought to complete unity. Then the world will know that you sent me and have loved them even as you have loved me.
>
> —JOHN 17:20-23

Paul wrote this:

> Make every effort to keep the unity of the Spirit through the bond of peace. There is one body and one Spirit, just as you were called to one hope when you were called; one Lord, one faith, one baptism; one God and Father of all, who is over all and through all and in all.
>
> —EPHESIANS 4:3-6

> If you have any encouragement from being united with Christ, if any comfort from his love, if any common sharing in the Spirit, if any tenderness and compassion, then make my joy complete by being like-minded, having the same love, being one in spirit and of one mind. Do nothing out of selfish ambition or vain conceit. Rather, in humility value

others above yourselves, not looking to your own
interests but each of you to the interests of others.

—Philippians 2:1–4

The bad news (again, these were my words from 2007)
is that our society is in terrible shape and we have either
failed to fight, fought the wrong battles, or fought with
the wrong weapons. The good news is that in Jesus we
have supernatural weapons—not of hatred or violence or
intimidation but of sacrificial, Spirit-empowered love—
and with these spiritual weapons we can change the world.

We are on the side of truth, and God is on the side of
the truth. What weapons can overthrow God and His
truth? Absolutely none!

It has been said that "Jesus transforms people, and people
transform society," and the bottom line is this: either we
will transform our society, or our society will transform us.
Which will it be?

Now take a deep breath, clear your head, and read
the previous paragraph once again, which represents the
closing words of my 2007 lecture. Think about what has
transpired from then until today, and then ask yourself
that closing question one more time: Which will it be?
Will society continue to change us, or will we change
society—through the power and truth of the gospel lived
out? Which will it be?

CHAPTER 4

THE PUSHBACK HAS CLEARLY BEGUN

O N June 24, 2022, the unthinkable happened. The Supreme Court, by a vote of 6–3, overturned *Roe v. Wade*, also undoing the subsequent and even worse decision of *Casey v. Planned Parenthood*. The infamous (and murderous) *Roe* decision had stood since 1973, while *Casey* had been enshrined since 1992, and in the eyes of most Americans there was no turning back after almost half a century with abortion on demand.

Surely a nation that took this for granted—this was one of the most fundamental, fiercely held "women's rights" in the land—would never allow something this essential to be overturned. It will never happen! But it did, and every day the reality of *Roe* becomes more and more of a distant memory as state after state pushes forward with pro-life legislation. Of course, the battle is still in its early stages, and the proabortion pushback is in full force as well. But even in the first months after the overturning of *Roe*, thousands of babies were saved.[1]

Yet those who were on the front lines of the pro-life movement in the early 1970s have told me that things seemed totally settled and fixed after the court's decision on *Roe*. The battle was lost. The nation had set its course, the pro-life movement was fragmented and discouraged, and pro-life leaders were hated and vilified even more than pro-family leaders are today. Yet the unthinkable took place, making America the only nation on the planet that went from nationally legalized abortion—in fact, our laws have been some of the most radical pro-abortion on the planet—to reversing that national trend, sending the decision back to the states. Ceaseless prayer, activism, political work, and messaging had their effect. Light has risen in the darkness.

But this is what many of us were expecting for years, with pro-life activists and intercessors looking forward to this very day. Prophetic dreams and words from the Lord assured us that *Roe* would come down, while the exhortation of Luke 18, to cry out for justice day and night, helped fuel the fires of the pro-life movement. And while I had dubbed 2022 the year of taking back ground, I did not realize at the beginning of that year that we would see such a momentous victory.

Yet this was only one of the major cultural battlefronts we have faced (and continue to face), and each of us has our particular calling and burden. In my case, beginning in 2004 the Lord called me to give special attention to LGBTQ+ activism, reaching out to the people with compassion while resisting the agenda with courage. In that respect too there were many landmark victories, with the pushback continuing into 2023, seen in particular during the Pride celebrations in June 2023, as many observers, both secular and religious, noticed that something felt different. More and more people were saying, "Enough already!" Even the pro-gay, liberal TV commentator Piers Morgan was crying foul, asking a gay comedian in the UK why *everything* had to be about gay and trans pride.[2] It was the very success of the gay revolution that was now leading to its undoing.[3]

As I wrote in 2015, "The gay revolution will continue to overplay its hand. As those who were once bullied now bully others, this will produce an increasing backlash....And as gay activists win more and more battles in the courts and the society, that will actually work against them, as their goals will continue to become more and more extreme."[4]

This has been self-evident for years. Or do you really think that a caring and sane society can tolerate more and more stories like this? "California woman, 18, sues doctors for removing her breasts when she was just THIRTEEN because she thought she was trans after seeing influencers online."[5]

That's why today, in 2024, I could point to secular websites that speak sympathetically about the growing "pushback against the perceived extreme expressions of gender fluidity."[6]

One headline asked (again, in a clearly pro-LGBTQ+ spirit), "Does 2023 Bring the Great Pushback Against LGBTQ+ Rights?"[7] These sentiments were reflected in headline after headline in 2023, reflecting the momentum that had been building in previous years:

- June 16, on the *Daily Wire*: "American Support for Same Sex Relations Dropped Seven Points Since Last Year."[8]

- June 8, on the *Daily Caller*: "The Left's Mass Deception About Gender Is Completely Failing, Major New Study Reveals. Left-wing ideas about gender are increasingly out of touch with American people of all generations and backgrounds, according to a new

poll by the nonpartisan Public Religion
Research Institute (PRRI)."[9]

- June 7, on the *Blaze*: "Parents livid over
  Pride video shown to 3rd, 4th, 5th graders in
  which child says, 'I never really felt like a
  boy, and I don't really feel like a girl, so I'd
  rather be both'"[10]

- June 13, on the Post Millennial: "'My
  Pronouns Are USA': Massachusetts middle
  school tries to make children wear rainbow
  clothing for Pride; students revolt, wear Red,
  White, and Blue."[11]

- June 15, on *USA Today*: "Social conservatism is on the rise. Maybe DeSantis is on to
  something with anti-'woke' fight. A new poll
  from Gallup found that 38% of Americans
  say they are conservative or very conservative
  on social issues—a nearly 30% increase since
  2021. Those identifying as liberals declined."[12]

- June 16, on the Daily Signal: "The Uprising:
  Families Clash With Schools Over LGBTQ
  Propaganda."[13]

- June 12, on the Stock Dork: "Uh-Oh! Pride
  Parades Get Thumbs Down From Americans:
  Is it Too Much Rainbow for Business?"[14]

- June 8, on Governing: "Storm Cloud
  Gathering Over Pride Month."[15]

- June 16, on MSN (from the *Washington Examiner*): "It's a shame what Pride has become."[16]

- June 13, on MSN (from Next Impulse Sports): "World reacts as transgender athletes are losing support in America."[17]

- June 14, on the Western Journal (from the Associated Press): "City Officially Bans 'Pride' Flags From Public Property, Tells LGBT Objectors 'You're Already Represented.'"[18]

- June 19, on The Stream: "The Uprising: Families Clash With Schools Over LGBTQ Propaganda."[19]

Quite a few articles in 2023 also focused on the striking news from an August Gallup poll that pointed to a dramatic spike in the rise of conservatism in America in the last two years. And so while only 10 percent of Democrats identified as conservative or very conservative (the same as in 2021), Independents moved from 24 to 29 percent, while Republicans moved from 60 to 74 percent. (Accordingly, Independents who identify as liberal or very liberal dropped in the previous two years from 27 to 23 percent.)

As for the breakdown by age, Gallup noted that "since 2021, there have been double-digit increases in conservative social ideology among middle-aged adults—those between the ages of 30 and 64. At the same time, older Americans' ideology on social issues has been stable, while there has been a modest increase in conservative social ideology among young adults."[20]

But even that "modest increase" was quite substantial, with eighteen-to-twenty-nine-year-olds who identify as conservative or very conservative moving from 24 to 30 percent in just two years. As for Americans between thirty and forty-nine years old, the shift was quite dramatic, from 22 to 35 percent, again, in just two years. This is highly significant.

As for views on same-sex relationships, Gallup observed that "last year, a record-high 71% of U.S. adults said gay or lesbian relations are morally acceptable. The figure has fallen back this year to 64%, returning to a level last seen in 2019."[21] Will that number continue to drop?

Also in 2023, as righteous laws were being passed in state after state to protect gender-confused children from radical surgery and irreversible drug treatments, for the first time in its forty-year history, the Human Rights Campaign, the world's largest LGBTQ+ activist organization, issued a national state of emergency.[22]

As I wrote in June 2023, I'm aware, of course, that the vast majority of LGBTQ+ identified readers will be either grieved or irate or shocked at the contents of this article. Even more will they be either grieved or irate or shocked by my attitude, as I'm quite pleased to see the shifts that I have highlighted here.

In their eyes (your eyes?), this is as hateful as it gets, an open and unashamed display of homophobia and transphobia, an unapologetic demonstration of the bigotry produced by fundamentalist religious beliefs.

Yes, I get it, and I understand your fear that I am celebrating the potential unraveling of what you have worked so hard to achieve over the last fifty years.[23]

The problem, of course, is that LGBTQ+ activists declared war on religion fifty years ago.

The problem is that their coming out of the closet necessitated putting us in the closet.

The problem is that they targeted our children with ceaseless indoctrination, from preschool to the university and from social media to TV and movies.

The problem is that the goalposts continued to move, and no recognition of "rights" was sufficient until the rights of those they opposed were removed.

The problem is that the trajectory of LGBTQ+ activism inevitably leads to queer critical theory, which denies the existence of human nature.

The problem is that the fringe elements of the community became celebrities.

The problem is that we will not stand by idly when our own kids or grandkids have been chemically castrated or genitally mutilated.

No way, nohow.

That's why I will continue to push back against what I truly believe is a destructive agenda for our society. At the same time, I will work against hatred and bigotry, seeking equal protection under the law for all and cultivating a climate of grace and mercy rather than anger and hatred.

Let us go about our work and live our lives as citizens in the same great country, even in the midst of our deep differences, and even as America, with God's help, turns back to at least a semblance of normalcy.

As I stated in my 2015 book, *Outlasting the Gay Revolution: Where Homosexual Activism Is Really Going and How to Turn the Tide*, "the call here is not so much to defeat the gay agenda as [much] as it is to promote a better agenda, one that by design will outlast the gay revolution."[24] By doing what is right and good, we will outlast what is wrong and harmful.

I pray that we will have the resolve to promote and live out that better agenda, especially now that the tide is clearly turning.[25]

Even Chadwick Moore, a "gay conservative," wrote, "Plenty has happened in the seven years since I was guillotined for coming out of the closet as a gay conservative. Whereas in 2016 only a handful seemingly existed, today thousands of LGBT influencers cram social-media feeds as part of a gathering wave rejecting the far-left. The result has been the alphabet mob's nose-dive into madness."[26] As I explained, the camel has gotten its toe in the door of the tent, and everything else has followed in its wake. As a result, millions of Americans are saying, "This is too much."[27] In the words of Allison Sullivan, this could be seen as "the Revolt of the Normies."[28]

As Joe Rogan said to his massive podcast audience, "So we're seeing that now where we never saw that before, where people are going 'Enough! Enough! Stop shoving this down everybody's throat....When I go to Target I don't want to see like [expletive] tuck pants, like they're designed to help you tuck your [expletive]. Hey, that's not normal, I don't want that right in front of everybody. It's weird."[29]

Similarly, nonconservative voices such as those of the famed scientist and atheist Richard Dawkins, the popular TV host and atheist Bill Maher, lesbian tennis great Martina Navratilova, and the mega-best-selling author of the Harry Potter series, J. K. Rowling (herself a longtime gay and lesbian ally), have joined together to push back against transgender activism, with Dawkins emphasizing that there are only two biological sexes and Rowling stating that only women, not men, can menstruate.[30]

In the same way, Maher, along with very secular voices such as those of singer Miley Cyrus, actress Sharon Stone, and Kelly Osbourne (daughter of the famous rocker Ozzie Osbourne), has been speaking out against cancel culture since 2021. The radical Left had gone too far, and even the broader society was crying foul.[31] By the end of 2023, in light of the shocking anti-Israel responses on major college campuses after the barbaric Hamas massacre of October 7, 2023, even liberal Jewish leaders were abandoning their alma maters, saying, "You will not get another dime from us." The destructive radicality of the "woke" educational agenda was plain for all to see.

But if we want to see real, deep, lasting societal change, *the church must lead the way.* Otherwise, if laws are passed without hearts being changed, those laws will soon be reversed. If people are put down rather than changed by the gospel, they will simply wait for the tables to turn when the oppressed can become the oppressors. If the conservative sector of the society gains greater power without demonstrating the kindness and compassion of Jesus, it will only increase resentment. If standards are raised primarily by human reasoning and societal preference without people encountering God for themselves, we will end up with a stiff, self-righteous legalism that will quickly crack and fall apart.

That's why it is essential that the moral and cultural revolution we so long to see is gospel based. That is the key to real, lasting transformation. Others who share many of our moral convictions but who are not born-again believers will certainly have their role to play, and in many cases it will be an important frontline role. But ultimately the church must lead the way if we want to see a real cultural transformation. We must go from revival to reformation. We must turn the tide!

Revival comes to set the church right, getting us back to God, back to the Word, back to the basics, back to solid families, back to worship, back to holiness, back to evangelism, back to ministries of compassion, back to righteousness, back to the Spirit. Now, with our light shining more brightly and our salt more freshly seasoned, we can fulfill our role in society. On with it!

PART II

THE BATTLE PLAN

CHAPTER 5

NEVER FORGET THAT OUR
MOST POWERFUL WEAPONS
ARE SPIRITUAL

THERE ARE TWO extremes we must avoid when working for cultural reformation. One is being entirely spiritual in our approach, relying only on prayer, fasting, and preaching the gospel while neglecting the many practical "earthly" things we can do as well. The other is putting all our emphasis on those practical "earthly" things (from feeding the poor to voting to getting involved in the school systems to being social media influencers) while neglecting the spiritual aspects of our calling. To emphasize only the spiritual side is to handicap our efforts; to neglect the spiritual side is to sabotage our efforts completely.

That's why I put this chapter toward the front of the book, since the foundation of all our work is spiritual, the most effective weapons we have are spiritual (and therefore supernatural), and the thing that sets us apart from the world is our spiritual—and very real—relationship with God. Everything we do must flow out of this Spirit-first emphasis. If we can keep this balance, then we can see radical change come.

These words of Jesus remind us of the utter folly of trying to accomplish God's work in human strength:

I am the true vine, and my Father is the vinedresser. Every branch in me that does not bear fruit he takes away, and every branch that does bear fruit he prunes, that it may bear more fruit. Already you are clean because of the word that I have spoken to you. Abide in me, and I in you. *As the branch cannot bear fruit by itself, unless it abides in the vine, neither can you, unless you abide in me. I am the vine; you are the branches. Whoever abides in me and I in him, he it is that bears much fruit, for apart from me you can do nothing.* If anyone does not abide in me he is thrown away like a branch and withers; and the branches are gathered, thrown into the fire, and burned. If you abide in me, and my words abide in you, ask whatever you wish, and it will be done for you. By this my Father is glorified, that you bear much fruit and so prove to be my disciples.

—John 15:1–8, esv, emphasis added

We would do well to meditate on these words regularly all the days of our lives. They are always on target and never get old.

Think back to Paul's letter to the Galatians. Although the context was very different from our current discussion, the question he asked them is quite relevant to us today: "Are you that stupid? Having begun with the Spirit's power, do you think you can reach the goal under your own power?" (Gal. 3:3, cjb). So if God by His Spirit fuels the fires of a powerful season of revival, giving us a vision to see our community (or city, or nation) changed, why do we think that we can now accomplish this goal by means of human effort alone?

When I first started teaching Bible school students in

the early 1980s, I often said to them, "When you're riding your bike up a steep climb and finally reach the place of descent, keep pedaling, since soon enough you'll hit another climb. You'll need all the momentum you can get."

So also, just as it is essential to remember the principle that the prayer that births the revival is the prayer that sustains the revival, so also it is that same focus in prayer that will birth and sustain the reformation. Otherwise, our best efforts will be either shortsighted, short-lived, short-circuited, or, worst of all, stillborn, going nowhere from the start.

Paul also had these important words to say; we know them well, but it's easy to lose sight of them:

> Finally, be strong in the Lord and in his mighty power. Put on the full armor of God, so that you can take your stand against the devil's schemes. For our struggle is not against flesh and blood, but against the rulers, against the authorities, against the powers of this dark world and against the spiritual forces of evil in the heavenly realms.
>
> —EPHESIANS 6:10–12

The Living Bible paraphrases verse 12:

> For we are not fighting against people made of flesh and blood, but against persons without bodies—the evil rulers of the unseen world, those mighty satanic beings and great evil princes of darkness who rule this world; and against huge numbers of wicked spirits in the spirit world.

Do we really believe this? Do we understand that ultimately it is not people we are fighting but demonic powers? That our issue is not so much with a political party or political agenda but with a satanic plan? And do we realize that the devil wants to destroy our ideological opponents as well, since he hates every human being with an unfathomable hatred? More importantly, do we realize that Jesus shed His blood for those very people—the ones whose words and actions grieve us so deeply—and that He wants to reach out to them to redeem them, just as He reached out to us? Is that our spiritual perspective?

Paul also wrote this:

> For though we live in the world [or in the flesh], we do not wage war as the world [or the flesh] does. The weapons we fight with are not the weapons of the world [or of the flesh]. On the contrary, they have divine power to demolish strongholds. We demolish arguments and every pretension that sets itself up against the knowledge of God, and we take captive every thought to make it obedient to Christ.
>
> —2 Corinthians 10:3–5

Or, to quote the paraphrase of verse 5 in *The Message*,

> we use our powerful God-tools for smashing warped philosophies, tearing down barriers erected against the truth of God, fitting every loose thought and emotion and impulse into the structure of life shaped by Christ.

God tools indeed! J. B. Phillips, in his expanded translation, put it like this (vv. 3–5):

> The truth is that, although of course we lead normal human lives, the battle we are fighting is on the

spiritual level. The very weapons we use are not those of human warfare but powerful in God's warfare for the destruction of the enemy's strongholds. Our battle is to bring down every deceptive fantasy and every imposing defence that men erect against the true knowledge of God. We even fight to capture every thought until it acknowledges the authority of Christ.

May we never lose sight of this important truth: "the battle we are fighting is on the spiritual level."

But remember, our battle is not *only* on the spiritual level, as if those of us fighting for the lives of starving children could just say to them, "Jesus is the bread of life! That's the only bread you need!" To the contrary, they need physical food for their physical well-being, and quoting scriptures to them will not ease their hunger. At the same time, they need spiritual food for their spiritual well-being. It is both-and, not either-or. But ultimately, in our efforts to function as the salt of the earth and the light of the world, we must never neglect the most effective weapons God has given us.

THIS IS HOW WE PULL DOWN STRONGHOLDS

Nothing in the universe is more powerful in changing circumstances than prayer. Nothing in the universe is more effective in changing lives than the gospel. And nothing in the universe bears more lasting fruit than making a true disciple. Nothing! That's why everything we do must be grounded in prayer, grounded in evangelism, grounded in disciple making. Everything we do must be grounded in setting captives free, in lifting up Jesus, in ministering in the anointing of the Spirit. Everything we do must flow out of the truth of God's unchangeable Word. This is how we win the battle. This is how we bring about lasting change. This is how we can see transformation come.

To be sure, we live in a fallen world, and it will remain fallen until Jesus returns. Even when we talk about America being saved, we don't mean that everyone will come to faith or that the whole nation will become Christian. And we certainly don't mean that our goal is to set up some kind of theocracy where we impose Christianity on the nation. Not for a moment.

Instead, we're saying that just as we have been heading in a very wrong direction for a full generation, we will make a major course correction. Just as there has been a steady spiritual and moral decline in America, that trend will be reversed. Ground will be taken back. Lives will be transformed. The downward, even freefall, slide will be arrested. Things will even get better. Marriages, and therefore families, will get stronger. Morals will rise. Spirituality will deepen. Civility will increase. Education will return to being more practical than ideological. These things can really happen!

But no amount of improved social agendas or "Get out the vote" campaigns or new soup kitchens or better rehab programs or improved educational incentives or godly business funding or Christian media takeovers can bring this about. The change must start in the heart. The transformation must be wrought by the Spirit. Everything else will either sink in the ocean of human sin or crash on the rocks of fleshly effort. The change must come from above, not below. That is the key to true reformation.

That's why, as we look at all the things we can do as godly reformers, we must remind ourselves that everything starts in prayer and that not only does God Himself hold the answers to our society's problems, but He Himself *is* the answer. We must never take our foot off the pedal of prayer! As author and evangelical lay minister S. D. Gordon (1859–1936) said, "Prayer is striking the winning blow....Service is gathering up the results."[1] Or, as Derek Prince (1915–2003) said, "Prayer is limitless. It's our intercontinental ballistic missile. We can launch it from anywhere and make it reach anywhere."[2] To go into battle without utilizing the power of prayer is to fight with both our hands tied behind our back and our feet shackled. (Actually, that's a massive understatement of the reality.) To use a contemporary analogy, it's like Iron Man going into battle against a supernatural opponent but forgetting to put on his Iron Man suit. To do so is to commit suicide.

We cannot neglect prayer if we want to see our nation changed—and that means prayer for our leaders, prayer for the salvation of sinners, prayer for the changing of hearts and minds, prayer for the spiritual vitality of our congregations, prayer for ourselves, and prayer that the Lord's name would be hallowed and His will done. This includes spiritual warfare and intercession. It includes fasting and self-denial. The ultimate battle is the battle of prayer.

I have no doubt that the early believers were praying for Saul of Tarsus, their arch persecutor. After all, Jesus had taught His followers to pray for those who persecuted them (see Matthew 5:44), and Acts tells us that Saul approved of the killing of Stephen and that he "began to destroy the church. Going from house to house, he dragged off both men and women and put them in prison" (Acts 8:1, 3). Sometime later, Acts records, "Saul was still breathing out murderous threats against the Lord's disciples. He went to the high priest and asked him for letters to the synagogues in Damascus, so that if he found any there who belonged to the Way, whether men or women, he might take them as prisoners to Jerusalem" (Acts 9:1–2).

I can't imagine that the believers were not praying for this violent enemy of their faith, a man who later said of himself, "I was once a blasphemer and a persecutor and a violent man" (1 Tim. 1:13). Yet this man became the writer of almost half the New Testament and one of the most influential spiritual leaders who ever lived. Who knows how many people like Saul/Paul are in our midst today—fanatical practitioners of other religions; famous actors or singers; political leaders; mega-wealthy, openly godless businessmen; influential intellectuals; radical revolutionaries—who will be dramatically converted in answer to our prayers, becoming unashamed champions of the faith.

And that ties in with another weapon we have that is far more powerful than anything the enemy can wield—more powerful than pornography and sexual temptation, more powerful than drugs and alcohol, more powerful than carnal prosperity and pride, more powerful than fear and intimidation. I'm talking about the power of the gospel, the power that can turn a sinner into a saint and a child of the devil into a child of God, the power that turns the arch-persecutor of the early church into the greatest apostle, the power than turns terrorists into Bible teachers and witches into soul winners and abortion activists into champions of life, the power that makes enemies into evangelists and foes into friends. That is the power of the gospel!

It was that same power that took me from LSD to PhD; from a rebellious, heroin-shooting, foulmouthed, evil-hearted sixteen-year-old Jewish hippie rock drummer to a Jesus-honoring, Word-loving, holy-living young man, all in a matter of weeks. And I am only one of hundreds of millions of others. Jesus really does save. The Spirit really does transform. That's why the weapon of Spirit-empowered evangelism is what sets us apart from the world.

I once heard the story of a man of God who was visiting a missionary colleague in Africa. The colleague asked him if he would like to meet the most powerful witch doctor in the community, and he was very happy to do so. The two of them walked into the witch doctor's dwelling and began to talk. The man of God said to him, "I understand that there is a very powerful spirit that works through you." The witch doctor said, "Yes, that is true." The man of God asked him, "Where is that spirit now?" The witch doctor replied, "He left when you came in." That is the power of the gospel.

It is true that in many ways America has become post-Christian and we can no longer take for granted certain values and beliefs. As my good friend professor Darrell Bock says, "In the old days, we used to tell people, 'It's true because it's in the Bible.' Today we need to tell them, 'It's in the Bible because it's true.'" The foundations have been shaken, and the whole building is tottering.

But that only underscores the readiness of the harvest. America is ripe for saving! A new Jesus People movement is urgently needed. The time for a massive wave of fresh evangelism is now![3] Let gospel preachers flood the country, from street corners to tents and from pulpits to the internet, and let a spirit of soul winning, of one-on-one, relational evangelism return. Let sharing the gospel become a way of life for us. Let winning the lost become our passion. And may we recover a true gospel message, not the contemporary "What's in it for me?" American version of the gospel, which is really no gospel at all. May we see true converts, born out of true conviction, birthed in the Spirit, changed from deep within, whom we help make into solid, clearheaded, Jesus-centered, deeply grounded, cross-bearing, spiritually minded, compassion-filled disciples. Who can oppose an army like this?

My longtime friend Larry Tomczak cited recent polling data that indicated

- with 400,000 churches in America, 80 per-cent are either stagnant or declining,

- among the remaining 20 percent, most church growth (about 95 percent) is biolog-ical or transfer,

- conversion growth is minimal, and

- stats are now more sobering, with many youths departing, falling prey to "deconstructionism."[4]

Isn't this then the key to turning America—seeing the people in our churches revived so that they in turn could touch the nation? Can you imagine how effective we would become as salt and light? Can you envision how great the national transformation would be with an on-fire church and multiplied millions of new converts who became solid disciples?

AN ARMY OF FAITH

Finally, in all that we do, we must never forget that we are people of faith—not fantasy, where we deny reality and believe in the delusions of our mind; not human optimism, where we think we can overcome real demonic strongholds with positive thinking; and not presumption, where we decide to take action on our own, apart from divine initiative. Instead, we are people of faith, like Moses, who "chose to be mistreated along with the people of God rather than to enjoy the fleeting pleasures of sin. He regarded disgrace for the sake of Christ as of greater value than the treasures of Egypt, because he was looking ahead to his reward. By faith he left Egypt, not fearing the king's anger; he persevered because he saw him who is invisible" (Heb. 11:25–27).

As Paul said, we endure hardship and opposition without flinching because "we fix our eyes not on what is seen, but on what is unseen, since what is seen is temporary, but what is unseen is eternal" (2 Cor. 4:18). Nothing can shake our holy confidence in our Lord. Nothing can lessen our resolve, because we are not moved by what we see or feel but rather by who God is and by what He has promised us. Fear has no place in our lives!

That's why we ground our praying and our proclaiming in a spirit of faith, as Paul also wrote (quoting from Psalm 116:10), "It is written: 'I believed; therefore I have spoken.' Since we have that same spirit of faith, we also believe and therefore speak, because we know that the one who raised the Lord Jesus from the dead will also raise us with Jesus and present us with you to himself" (2 Cor. 4:13–14). We too know that Jesus died for our sins and rose triumphant from the grave. We know that the light shines in the darkness and that the darkness cannot overcome it (John 1:5). We know that in the end Jesus will return and establish His kingdom here on earth, doing away with wickedness and establishing a world of justice and honor. This is what we believe, and this is why we also speak.

It is these eternal realities that infuse us with faith every single day, no matter what comes our way. It is the truth of God and His Word, the truth of the Spirit and the resurrection, the truth of the lordship of Jesus that help us look beyond the pain and the failures and the setbacks and the injustices of the hour, causing us to shout instead, "We believe God!"

The resurrected Jesus said, "All authority in heaven and on earth has been given to me" (chew on those words for a moment; let their reality settle in) before He said, "Therefore go and make disciples of all nations, baptizing them in the name of the Father and of the Son and of the Holy Spirit, and teaching them to obey everything I have commanded you." And it was that same risen Jesus who closed the Great Commission with these words: "And surely I am with you always, to the very end of the age" (Matt. 28:18–20). Is that not more than enough for us?

We might suffer setbacks for a season. We might see the tide keep turning in the wrong direction in our neighborhoods or schools or state legislatures. We might see an ongoing moral, spiritual, and cultural decline, right in the midst of our praying and preaching. And yet if God has given us a promise, just as He promised the overturning of *Roe* to some faithful pro-life leaders and intercessors, we are undaunted. We believe God! And that spirit of faith within us will become contagious, encouraging others to stand up and make their proclamation as well. "We believe God too!"

People often ask me how I remain so confident and faith-filled with all the unrelenting bad news I write about and talk about daily. I tell them, "The same God who showed me that things would get worse also promised me that the tide would turn if we obeyed His calling!" And so the bad news, as painful as it is for the moment and as grievous as it is to watch, also brings me encouragement. The storm has been predicted, but so has the fair weather that will follow.

It was this same spirit of faith that empowered Joshua and Caleb. They too saw the giants in the land. They too knew the obstacles were severe. But they also knew that this was *promised land*—God Himself had given His Word—and so despite all the challenges they declared, "We can take the land!" (See Numbers 13:30.) It was this same spirit of faith that carried many a missionary pioneer who labored in obscurity for years, seeing very little fruit. Today we look back at them as heroes, and we are stunned to see the results of their work.

Hudson Taylor (1832–1905), the famed missionary to China, said, "We are a supernatural people; born again by a supernatural birth; we wage a supernatural fight and are taught by a supernatural teacher; led by a supernatural captain to assured victory."[5] David Livingstone (1813–1873), the famed missionary to Africa, said, "On the following words I staked everything, and they never failed, 'Lo, I am with you always, even unto the end of the world.'"[6] And it was the famed evangelist D. L. Moody (1837–1899) who is credited with saying, "What a difference in the men who go into battle intending to conquer *if they can*, and those who go into battle intending to conquer."[7] In the words of Puritan leader William Gurnall (1616–1679), best known for his work *The Christian in Complete Armour*, "Let the devil choose his way; God is a match for him at every weapon. The devil and his whole council are but fools to God; nay, their wisdom foolishness."[8] How true!

That same spirit of faith empowers us to march forward, believing for a massive harvest of souls, a fresh outpouring of the Spirit, a sustained revival in the church, a sweeping cultural awakening, a growing nationwide consciousness of God, and the exaltation of Jesus' name, knowing that as we do what is right in the sight of God and live in the light of eternity, His Word will not return void. We believe God!

As 1 John declares, "For everyone born of God overcomes the world. This is the victory that has overcome the world, even our faith. Who is it that overcomes the world? Only the one who believes that Jesus is the Son of God" (1 John 5:4–5). In Jesus we overcome—whether people revere us or revile us, celebrate us or crucify us, receive us or reject us; whatever comes our way, we overcome. That is who we are. We believe God!

It is in that same spirit of faith that I have written this book, not simply as a theoretical exercise that is doomed to fail nor as a book that will not age well. To the contrary, I truly believe what I am writing in this book because I truly believe that God has called me to write it—because I truly believe that we will see an awakening.

As surely as we are living with the disastrous effects of the counterculture revolution that began in the 1960s, so too we will see a holy pushback, a new Jesus Revolution, and in front of our eyes the tide will turn. I believe God!

The first task then must always remain the primary task: the church must be the church. Everything else will flow from that. As evangelist Joe Oden asked, "What would the communities of the West look like if the chief activity of local ministry leaders was prayer and proclamation? What would it look like if ministry leaders gave as much time to prayer as they do administration? I submit we would have what the early church had. A cultural revolution."[9]

CHAPTER 6

LOVING YOUR NEIGHBOR AS YOURSELF

THE WRITERS OF the New Testament often called us to demonstrate our faith by our good deeds. As Jesus said, "Let your light shine before others, that they may see your good deeds and glorify your Father in heaven" (Matt. 5:16). When people see the way we live and the way we care about others, they will give glory to God.[1] In the words of a classic song from the 1960s, "they'll know we are Christians by our love"—our love for one another and our love for the people of this world. It is hard to argue with love.

Jesus called for this kind of love over and over again, illustrating it vividly in His famous parable of the good Samaritan (where the unlikely hero of the story was a despised outsider who cared for a badly injured Jew; see Luke 10). He also taught this:

> When you give a luncheon or dinner, do not invite
> your friends, your brothers or sisters, your relatives,
> or your rich neighbors; if you do, they may invite
> you back and so you will be repaid. But when you
> give a banquet, invite the poor, the crippled, the
> lame, the blind, and you will be blessed. Although

> they cannot repay you, you will be repaid at the resurrection of the righteous.
>
> —LUKE 14:12–14

What a lofty ethic!

The Lord even said that on the day when He judges the nations, the difference between the sheep and the goats will be their sacrificial care for "the least of these"—and that care included feeding the hungry, giving drink to the thirsty, taking in the destitute, giving clothes to those who had none, caring for the sick, and visiting the prisoners (see Matthew 25:31–46). And while there has always been debate about who exactly Jesus meant when He spoke of "the least of these," there is no debate that this sacrificial love became a trademark of the church through the centuries. This reflects the heart of God.

That's why the early Christians were known for their compassionate care for the poor and the sick. As Pastor Tim Keller noted, "While it was expected to care for the poor of one's family or tribe, Christians' 'promiscuous' help given to all poor—even of other races and religions, as taught in Jesus's parable of the Good Samaritan (Luke 10:25–37)—was unprecedented....During the urban plagues, Christians characteristically didn't flee the cities but stayed and cared for the sick and dying of all groups, often at the cost of their own lives."[2]

One scholar suggested that Jesus, and not Hippocrates, should be viewed as the "father of medicine" since Jesus "was more often engaged in acts of healing than in almost anything else...[and it] was the humble Galilean who more than any other figure in history bequeathed to the healing arts their essential meaning and spirit."[3] And the medical historian H. E. Sigerist wrote, "It remained for Christianity to introduce the most revolutionary and decisive change in the attitude of society toward the sick. Christianity came into the world as the religion of healing, as the joyful Gospel of the Redeemer and of Redemption. It addressed itself to the disinherited, to the sick and afflicted and promised them healing, a restoration both spiritual and physical." Thus, "it became the duty of the Christian to attend to the poor and the sick of the community."[4]

Not surprisingly, a twentieth-century Christian physician wrote,

> Early in my manhood I said I could not be a physician unless I were first a disciple of Jesus Christ.... *Jesus healed.* It follows that the gospel of Jesus cannot be complete without that compassionate ministry. Jesus demonstrated that our God is compassionate, that He is moved by human suffering. And therefore Christ's disciples must seek to be instruments of healing, in one or more of the various avenues available for medical ministry. Christian medicine must be above all else an exhibit, a demonstration, of the character of God."[5]

We love because He loved us. We love because He *is* love.[6]

CREATED IN THE IMAGE OF GOD

Christians were also moved by their belief that all human beings are created in the image of God and therefore deserving of kindness and compassion. As noted by historian Gary Ferngren, "Early Christian philanthropy was deeply informed by the theological concept of the *imago Dei*, that humans were created in the image of God—a belief that Christianity had taken over from Judaism." And it was this concept, Ferngren writes, that "was to have four important consequences for practical ethics that became increasingly apparent as Christianity began to penetrate the world of the Roman Empire. Together they represent a radical departure from the social ethics of classical paganism." How exactly did this work itself out?

> The first was the impetus that the doctrine gave to Christian charity and philanthropy. The classical world had no religious or ethical impulse for individual charity. Personal concern for the poor and needy was an important theme in the Hebrew Scriptures, which gave rise to the insistence in later Judaism that almsgiving is a duty and even the highest virtue.
>
> This emphasis was appropriated by Christianity and is mentioned often in the pages of the New Testament, where charity is represented as an outgrowth of *agape*, which is rooted in the nature of God. Just as God loved humans, so they were expected to respond to divine love by extending love to his brother, who bore the image of God (John 13:34–35). Love of God and devotion to Christ provided the motivation for love of others that had its practical outworking in charity (Matthew 25:34–40). Compassion was regarded as a manifestation of Christian love (Colossians 3:12; 1 John 3:17) and an essential element of the Christian's obligation to all people.[7]

Ferngren explains that "a second consequence of the doctrine of the *imago Dei* was that it provided the basis for the belief that every human life has absolute intrinsic value as a bearer of God's image and as an eternal soul for whose redemption Christ died." He further states, "A third consequence of the doctrine of the *imago Dei* was in providing early Christians with a new perception of the body, and indeed of the human personality." Finally, "a fourth consequence was that the doctrine of the *imago Dei* led to a redefinition of the poor. The human body in all its parts shared in the divine image. This was true, not merely of the bodies of Christians, but of all men. It was true particularly of the poor, who acquired a new definition in Christian thought: those who had true worth because they bore the face (*prosopon*) of Christ."[8]

This last point reminds me of a story I heard about a godly American missionary who had given her life to the poorest of the poor in Africa. In a vision she heard the Lord say to her, "Come up here with Me, where the poor are." Yes, the poor were "up there," with Jesus. In His eyes they were highly esteemed. How different are God's eyes than ours!

THIS IS ONE MAJOR WAY THAT WE CHANGE THE WORLD

One of the most important ways we can bring about lasting cultural change is by caring for the poor, loving the unloved, and reaching out to the marginalized, thereby providing tangible help in our local communities and beyond. Thankfully, this is one area where the church has led the way for centuries, both in America and abroad. We have built hospitals. We have fed and clothed innumerable orphans. We have sent out wave after wave of medical teams. We have paid for the digging of wells. We have improved the quality of life for the impoverished living in far-off places. We have raised up schools and pioneered educational institutions. We have rescued children and adults sold into sex slavery.

Countless churches are known for their services to their communities, providing rehab programs for addicts, marital counseling for troubled couples, soup kitchens for the hungry, and so much more. As a result, when these same churches get bad press because of their moral and cultural stands, the people in their communities often speak up on their behalf. "Hey, I know these people, and they're good people. They helped clean up our neighborhood. They help our kids. Don't be saying bad things about them."

So just as prayer, evangelism, and discipleship are the foundation for everything we do, so also are acts of compassion part of that foundation. This too is an essential part of the gospel. This too is how we make God known to the world. But we can only do this effectively if we really care. In other words, this is a ministry, not a method; an expression of love, not an effective technique.

One of my closest friends in the world is an Indian brother named Yesupadam. He was raised as an untouchable in India, almost dying of malnutrition as a boy. (A Canadian missionary found him lying on the side of the road and took him to a hospital, where he was nursed back to health.) As he grew older, he developed a hatred for the caste system and became a radical Maoist communist (called a Naxalite) at the age of eleven, signing his pledge in his own blood and engaging in acts of violence against the rich.

He was going to change the world. He was going to be a revolutionary. Instead, by the time he was in his twenties, he was a lost alcoholic atheist. And then Jesus appeared to him, revealing His great love, and Yesupadam was instantly transformed, going right onto the streets to proclaim the good news: Jesus was real!

After serving in different capacities in several churches, he launched his own ministry, Love-N-Care. And how did he start? He took in orphans, providing them with shelter, three meals a day, and a Christian education. He also started doing evangelistic outreaches and planting churches. But his care for "the least of these" was where everything started. He knew what it was to have nothing. He knew what it was to experience starvation, day in and day out, for years. He knew the injustice of the caste system. And now, finally, through the gospel he understood the Jesus way to change the world. My friend has become a holy revolutionary!

Over the years, his ministry has trained workers who have planted more than ten thousand churches in unreached tribal villages. (At least five of these church planters have been martyred over the years; most have been physically attacked at one time or another.) And where these churches have been planted—in the midst of extreme poverty—the standard of living has also risen. Yesupadam's ministry also cares for the elderly and the mentally ill, as well as providing specialized training for those who are physically handicapped. And remarkably, he has been able to replicate his work in other countries, even in post-Christian Europe!

In each case he starts by reaching out to the poor in tangible ways, making clear that he and his team are doing this because of Jesus. The results have been nothing short of remarkable. But here is the point that you must hear: he does not do all this to get results. He does it because he cares. The results follow naturally.

This deeply challenges many of us (certainly me!),

especially here in America, where we can be so results-oriented and often pour ourselves primarily into the successful, ministering to the movers and shakers while neglecting those who seem to have little to offer. May the Lord forgive us! May He change our hearts! And while it's also critically important that we minister to the movers and shakers (we'll talk about that throughout this book), it's even more critical that we have God's heart. After all, He's the One who gives the increase, and without His blessing we can do nothing.

As for the results that follow our heartfelt acts of service, they will speak for themselves. In fact, to give an extreme example, if you have ever wondered why a terrorist organization like Hamas can be so popular among Palestinians, it's because Hamas has two wings. One is the military wing, which is popular among the people because in their eyes it is waging war against the Israeli infidels. The other wing of Hamas is devoted to providing social welfare programs to the people, also overseeing their schools and hospitals.

As a Wikipedia article correctly summarizes,

> Hamas developed its social welfare programme by replicating the model established by Egypt's Muslim Brotherhood. For Hamas, charity and the development of one's community are both prescribed by religion and to be understood as forms of resistance. In Islamic tradition, *dawah* (lit. transl. "the call to God") obliges the faithful to reach out to others by both proselytising and by charitable works, and typically the latter center on the mosques which make use of both [official Islamic] endowment resources and charitable donations (*zakat*, one of the five pillars of Islam) to fund grassroots services like

nurseries, schools, orphanages, soup kitchens, women's activities, library services and even sporting clubs within a larger context of preaching and political discussions. In the 1990s, some 85% of its budget was allocated to the provision of social services.[9]

This of course does not minimize the barbaric evil nature of Hamas' terrorist activities. But it does provide insight into the popularity of Hamas on the grassroots level. It is not just that the Hamas operatives are perceived as freedom fighters. They are also perceived as people who care about their communities in tangible ways. How much more can Christians lead the way here!

Do you remember what I wrote about Finney's impact in Rochester, New York, from 1829–30? The journalist who told the story for *Reader's Digest* noted that among Finney's converts were "lawyers, doctors, judges, tradesmen, bankers, boatmen, workers, master craftsmen." But Finney did not simply tell them how to "get saved" and enjoy a blessed life in the here and now and then eternal life forever. Instead, he "scorched their consciences and urged them not to follow the selfish ways of the world. Finney angrily denounced the evils of selfishness and deliberately aimed his message at the wealthy and powerful." Then, with these wealthy people soundly converted, "Finney's final step was to get them to direct their energy and wealth into beneficial philanthropies."[10]

Can we follow that model today? Can we too prioritize these ministries of compassion? Can we too encourage generosity toward the poor and hurting? Without question, American Christians are known for their generosity worldwide, and I have been deeply blessed to meet many

Christian businessmen who are models of charity and care. So let us redouble our efforts and continue to take ground in the process.

And in a society increasingly marked by racial tension and division, let us not divide along partisan political lines or, worse, along racial or ethnic lines. Instead, let us pursue genuine understanding, give ourselves to acts of righteousness, stand for justice, and unify around Jesus our Lord. In His eyes, the body is not divided along color lines, ethnic lines, economic lines, or educational lines. We are all one in Him, and as the world sees us truly caring for another, they will recognize us as the Lord's disciples. (See John 13:34–35.)

As we live the gospel out in our communities, loving our neighbors as ourselves, we will 1) glorify Jesus in their eyes as His representatives; 2) undo some of the damage created by our many schisms and scandals; 3) show everyday people what everyday Christians are all about; 4) help those in need, whether or not they respond to the gospel; and 5) bring many people to Jesus as they experience the love of God in action.

Writing in 1970, Francis Schaeffer articulated this vision of revolutionary Christianity:

> Hot Christianity: "First, for ourselves and for our spiritual children, we need a Christianity that is strong, one that is not just a memory. The games of yesterday are past. We are in a struggle that the church has never been in before."[11]

Compassionate Christianity: "Second, our Christianity must become truly universal, relevant to all segments of society and all societies of the world."[12]

Open Your Home for Community: "Don't start a big program. Don't suddenly think you can add to your church budget and begin. Start personally and start in your homes. I dare you. I dare you in the name of Jesus Christ. Do what I am going to suggest. Begin by opening your home for community."[13]

May the Lord give us His strategy and, more importantly, His heart. Love never fails!

CHAPTER 7

HAVING MORE BABIES IS ESSENTIAL, BUT THEN WHAT?

WHY IS ISLAM often considered to be the fastest-growing religion on the planet? High birth rates in Muslim families. Why is the nation of Israel becoming more and more right-wing? High birth rates in religious Jewish families. Why has India overtaken China as the world's most populous nation? Similar answer again: high birth rates in Hindu families.

In the case of Islam, "Muslim women have an average of 2.9 children, significantly above the next-highest group (Christians at 2.6) and the average of all non-Muslims (2.2). In all major regions where there is a sizable Muslim population, Muslim fertility exceeds non-Muslim fertility."[1]

As for Israel, while secular (and therefore more left-leaning) Israelis average 2 babies per woman, Orthodox Jewish Israelis (who lean strongly right) average 3.9 babies per woman, and ultra-Orthodox Jewish Israelis (who lean even more strongly right) average 6.6 babies per woman. Although this is not the only reason for Israel's shift to the right, it is a major reason. As explained by Israeli academic Dahlia Scheindlin, religiosity is the dominant predictive factor in how a young person will vote in Israel.[2]

As for India, which was never plagued by a one-child-per-family policy, as was China, and does not face some of the same social dynamics that discourage people from having more children,[3] the high birth rate has made all the difference. An article on the Economic Discussion website lists ten reasons for the high birth rates in India, including early and universal marriage, joint family systems, and the effect of religious beliefs, here meaning Hindu beliefs. The article states that "in India, religion plays a major role in large size families. A son is to provide continuity to family legacy. Even after so many girls in the family, the desire for one son prompts parents to continue with their child producing activity."[4] That's why I was not surprised when a Christian colleague of mine in India told me that in his opinion the most prized value in his country—the thing that is cherished the most—is family (in contrast with America, where most people would say that our most prized value is freedom/independence).[5]

Similarly, an Islamic website notes that

> the family is the foundation of Islamic society. The peace and security offered by a stable family unit is greatly valued and seen as essential for the spiritual growth of its members. It is quite common in the Muslim community to find large, extended families living together; providing comfort, security and support to one another.[6]

As for Judaism, an ultra-Orthodox website states, "Ever since G-d told Adam and Eve to be fruitful and multiply, Judaism has viewed having children as a holy enterprise, a partnership with G-d Himself. Among religious Jews, it is not uncommon for a couple to gladly birth and raise as many as they are blessed with."[7] In keeping with this, one of my friends with whom I have dialogued for years, an ultra-Orthodox rabbi living in New Jersey, has fourteen children. Yet he told me this is not uncommon in his community. They fully embrace the biblical teaching that children are a heritage from the Lord. (See Psalm 127:3–5.)

In the words of Moses Maimonides (1138–1204), "although a person has fulfilled the *mitzvah* [commandment] of being fruitful and multiplying [see Genesis 1:28; "be fruitful and multiply" is taken as a divine command in Judaism], he is bound by a Rabbinic commandment not to refrain from being fruitful and multiplying as long as he is physically potent, for anyone who adds a soul to the Jewish people is considered as if he built an entire world."[8] Yes, having children is a matter of world building in Judaism. This simple chart says it all.[9]

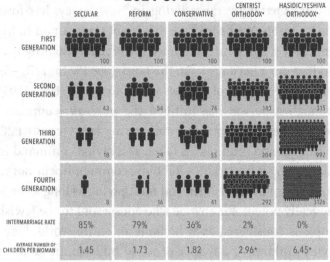

THE FUTURE OF AMERICAN JEWRY

Will Your Grandchild Be Jewish?
2021 UPDATE

	SECULAR	REFORM	CONSERVATIVE	CENTRIST ORTHODOX*	HASIDIC/YESHIVA ORTHODOX*
FIRST GENERATION	100	100	100	100	100
SECOND GENERATION	43	54	74	143	315
THIRD GENERATION	18	29	55	204	992
FOURTH GENERATION	8	16	41	292	3126
INTERMARRIAGE RATE	85%	79%	36%	2%	0%
AVERAGE NUMBER OF CHILDREN PER WOMAN	1.45	1.73	1.82	2.96*	6.45*

= 10 people. All categories represent **current** identification

• Although there is no clear definition of Centrist Orthodox or Hasidic/Yeshiva Orthodox, the main distinguishing factors relate to attitudes regarding formal secular studies, family size and the type of day school children attend.

* Statistics pertaining to fertility rates for Orthodox were based primarily on data extrapolated by Dr. Marvin Schick ("A Census of Jewish Day Schools in the United States, 2013–2014," October 2014).[10]

CONSERVATIVES HAVE MORE KIDS THAN LIBERALS, BUT...

This is not just an emphasis in Islam, Hinduism, and Judaism. As a July 2021 headline in the Western Journal announced, "Birth Rates Are the Right's Secret Weapon as Liberal Values Backfire."[11] The article stated that "data from the General Social Survey indicates that in the 1970s 'there was little or no difference in fertility rates between liberal and conservative women,' according to the Institute for Family Studies."

Over time, though, that statistic has changed dramatically, and the author reported, "As of 2018, the gap had widened markedly, with conservative women between the ages of 30–44 averaging near 2.5 children and liberal women just over 1.5." She continued, "To approach the data another way, the survey also shows that a random sample of 100 conservative adults will raise 208 children. One hundred liberal adults will raise only 147 kids, according to Fatherly."

And what does this mean in practical terms? The author stated, "That gap means that conservatives could hold a political edge, as the size of liberal families continues to dwindle. The evidence that supports this idea is overwhelming."[12]

As noted by Religion Unplugged on October 4, 2021, in America, "the group that is the least likely to have children are atheists and agnostics. They hit peak fertility around 42 years old, when about 40% of them have children. It's noteworthy that, according to this data, potentially half of atheists and agnostics never reproduce. Thus, for these groups to grow, they have to rely on conversion more than retention."[13]

The Fatherly website noted that

> liberals are not having enough babies to keep up with conservatives. Arthur Brooks, a social scientist at Syracuse University, was the first to point this out all the way back in 2006 when he went on *ABC News* and blew blue staters minds. "The political Right is having a lot more kids than the political Left," he explained. "The gap is actually 41 percent." Data on

the U.S. birth rate from the General Social Survey confirms this trend—a random sample of 100 conservative adults will raise 208 children, while 100 liberal adults will raise a mere 147 kids. That's a massive gap.[14]

These are very striking, consequential observations. But they are not surprising observations. That's because the great majority of atheists and agnostics lean left politically and ideologically, putting them in the proabortion, pro-same-sex-marriage category—in other words, in a category that does not put the same emphasis on procreation as does the pro-life, pro-natural marriage category. In addition, those leaning to the left are often more pessimistic about the future due to fears of catastrophic global warming or other end-of-the-world scenarios, because of which they are less inclined to bring children into the world. That's why the Religion Unplugged article was titled "The Future of American Religion: Birth Rates Show Who's Having More Kids."

An article posted on August 8, 2022, by the Institute for Family Studies (Pew) reinforces these observations.

Birth rates in the United States are near record lows, but not for everyone. Indeed, under the surface of the fertility decline since 2007 is a little noticed fact: fertility has declined much more among nonreligious Americans than among the devout. Data from the National Survey of Family Growth (NSFG) from 1982 to 2019, along with data from four waves of the Demographic Intelligence Family Survey (DIFS) from 2020 to 2022, point to a widening gap in fertility rates between more religious and less religious

Americans. In recent years, the fertility gap by religion has widened to unprecedented levels.[15]

The author then added a major caveat in terms of the *retention rate* of the children religious people are having: we are having more babies, but many of our children, as they grow up, are leaving the faith. (This is the reason for the "but" in the chapter title.) As a critic posted on our AskDrBrown YouTube channel, "The reason Xianity is still growing—along with atheism—is demographics. Xians have more kids. But give every child a college-level education and internet access and watch Xianity die out!"[16] As exaggerated as this comment was, it was not without some basis in fact.

So on the positive side, "the more frequently Americans attend religious services, the more children they will have, on average. The less frequently they attend religious services, the less children they will have, on average. Even in 2015, Pew Research could report that evangelicals and Catholics averaged 2.3 children per family (Mormons averaged 3.4) while atheists averaged 1.6 children per family and agnostics 1.3 children."[17] These are significant, undeniable disparities. But they don't tell the whole story.

As the Institute for Family Studies (Pew) notes, "while this difference may comfort some of the faithful who hope higher fertility will ultimately yield stable membership in churches and synagogues, these hopes may be in vain. Rates of conversion into irreligion are too high, and fertility rates too low, to yield stable religious populations." Yes, "despite a widening fertility gap, the ongoing trend of younger Americans becoming more secular more than offsets the fertility advantage enjoyed by religious people."[18] Please stop for a moment and read those words again. They really do cut to the heart.

Consequently, "religious communities in America will tend to decline by about 25% in each generation. If these trends continue, then within three generations (that is, by the time current children in churches are elderly grandparents), religious communities in America will have shrunk by more than half, a devastating loss." And then, for the real kicker: "On the other hand, nonreligious Americans need to only have 0.8 to 0.9 children, on average, to achieve population growth, given their conversion rates: in fact, they currently have 1.3 children, implying 50-60% population growth every generation."[19]

The solution then is threefold: 1) As God leads and provides, we should continue to have larger families than do secular Americans. (Please stay with me here even if you say, "That's not for me." I am *not* here to judge or legislate, let alone to play God.) 2) With God's help, we must find a better way to get our kids grounded in the faith so that the great majority do not fall away. (Please don't feel condemned if your kids are not walking with the Lord. We'll revisit each of these points in depth—and with compassion.) 3) We increase our Spirit-empowered efforts to win and disciple the lost (as outlined in chapter 5), as well as do our best to win back those who have left the faith, especially those closest to us. This threefold plan of attack, with the help of the Lord, can bring about a massive shift in the spiritual and moral fabric of America over the next thirty to forty years.

FOCUS ON THE CHILDREN

Before we get into this subject any deeper, it's important that I speak with complete candor. The last thing I want is for anyone reading these words to feel judged or condemned, especially by me. That's because Nancy and I had two kids, not three, let alone six or ten, and it never occurred to us to devote serious time to seeking the Lord about how many children He wanted us to have. (For those couples who have been unable to have children of your own, may He make a way for you to be the parents of many!)

We had our two daughters within the first thirty-three months of marriage; then we began taking in Vietnamese and Cambodian refugees, including a couple with their baby, as well as single men, then an American baby, then the baby's mother. After a number of years, when we no longer had any refugees or needy Americans living in our home, our daughters were a little older, and it just felt as if this was our family. We never really thought about having more kids. Now, as we're nearing seventy, it's a moot question!

I've also observed over the years that some sincere Christians felt a mandate to have as many babies as possible, but they didn't have a support structure to help them (such as a mom or mother-in-law nearby or a circle of friends who could help out where needed). As a result, in some cases the marriages came under intense pressure—and even fell apart—as moms got run down, dads got overwhelmed, and children got neglected. How then did this glorify the Lord or advance His cause on the earth?

Thankfully, I know many families with lots of kids, and the marriages are strong, the moms and dads are doing well individually and as couples, and the children are thriving. Praise God! But again, I'm not here to point a finger or bring an accusation of any kind. Nor am I saying that every couple is called to have at least X number of children.[20] What I am saying is 1) we should cultivate a biblical mentality that celebrates babies and children (you might want to meditate on Psalms 127–128); 2) we should honor the high callings of motherhood and fatherhood; and 3) as married couples in our childbearing years, we should ask the Lord for His plan in terms of having children.[21] All that being said, it's one thing to have more children. It's another thing to have more children who grow up to love the Lord and love what is right. That's where the rubber meets the road. And so putting aside the positive stats regarding higher birth rates among believers, the next question must be, "Who is doing a better job of indoctrinating the next generation, the church or the world?" As stated earlier in this chapter, "despite a widening fertility gap [between the non-religious and the religious], the ongoing trend of younger Americans becoming more secular more than offsets the fertility advantage enjoyed by religious people."[22]

Here too I am not pointing a condemning finger. I'm sure plenty of men reading this book were (and are) better fathers than I was, not to mention better husbands. And while Nancy and I have been married for forty-eight years now (we are deeply in love and enjoy tremendous harmony in our marriage), and while we have wonderful relationships with our daughters and their spouses, along with our amazing grandchildren, I have never thought of myself as a Father of the Year candidate. Other fathers put me to shame. I could have been much more focused and present as a father, even if overall I was very serious about raising our kids as a loving, God-fearing dad.

I'm simply addressing an urgent need here in the most truthful and straightforward way I can, without bringing an accusation against others. There *is* an all-out assault on our kids, the likes of which no generation has ever seen before. And as much as Nancy and I did our best to keep negative influences out of the home (as our daughters were growing up, we didn't even have a TV), the challenge has intensified exponentially since then.

THINGS ARE WORSE THAN WE IMAGINE

About ten years ago I was speaking at a church in California with seven thousand to eight thousand members. It was a vibrant, soul-winning congregation that believed in preaching the Word and making disciples. Yet the executive pastor shared something with me with a heavy heart. He said that none of his children, all of whom were young adults, agreed with him or the church when it came to homosexual relationships. They were all raised in the faith, raised in church, raised in a stable home with a healthy marriage. Yet none of them embraced what the Scriptures clearly teach on homosexuality. How could this be? It appears that the world did a better job of discipling them than their church and family did.

More recently, a mother contacted me in great distress. My wife and I had known her since she was a little girl. Now she was living overseas, her husband was a pastor, and they were devoted parents who were very much involved with their kids. Yet their oldest daughter, whom we'll call Rachel, had begun to identify as transgender, quite out of the blue, around the age of sixteen.

After this happened, our friend and her husband learned

that the high school Rachel attended was about to announce that she was now a "he." The parents only found this out because they had made an appointment to speak with counselors at the school about the sudden changes in Rachel's behavior. That's when they discovered that the school had been encouraging Rachel's trans identity and was about to make the big announcement the very next day, without notifying the parents. In fact, the school was giving Rachel information on how she could be removed from the home if her parents were not affirming. This is madness.

Before this, Rachel had been mildly autistic but, as far as her sexuality, very girlish. Now everything changed, and the parents were absolutely mystified. What happened to their daughter? Once she turned eighteen and left the home, things quickly degenerated, and the mother's emails became more outraged and broken.

In 2022 she sent me a video by Matt Walsh titled "TikTok Is Making Mental Illness Trendy."[23] Walsh noted how destructive ideas and behavior and concepts "can go from fringe to trendy to mainstream quite literally overnight." He added, "What was unusual one moment might be ubiquitous the next, and people, especially young people, can get caught in the current and drowned before they even notice that their shoes are wet."

He pointed to the latest TikTok fascination with what is called multiple personality disorder (MPD), as a result of which large numbers of young people are wrongly diagnosing themselves with this unusual (and controversial) condition. He played a clip from *Good Morning America*, where this phenomenon was discussed with real concern, as the host noted that videos with hashtags like #Dissociativeidentitydisorder and

#Borderlinepersonalitydisorder have been viewed hundreds of millions of times. This really has become epidemic.

Walsh then explained that the young person who self-diagnoses with MPD refers to himself or herself as "the system," with each personality within "the system" being called an "alter." And what effect does this have on young people? Here's what Rachel's mom wrote. You can feel her anguish in every word:

> Do you know anything about this??? I'm literally livid. This is how it started with us. Rachel went on some social media site, convinced herself she was a system with lots of personalities, like 100. And did this exact same thing!! When I spoke to the psychiatrists about this, they had no clue what I was talking about. No one has been helpful with this. Why is no one talking about this?!?! I'm so angry right now. Part of what the issue is with Rachel, she thinks she has several alters with all different genders. Why would any doctor give her testosterone acting like this?

So trained psychiatrists had not heard about this destructive TikTok trend, but millions of impressionable young people were intimately familiar with it. And here in America, where the daughter now resides, a licensed doctor was willing to give this teenager a testosterone shot to help her "transition" to male, even though her mental instability should have been visible at once.

The mother continued, "She is so wrapped up and so deep in lies, I don't know how to bring her to truth....Her roommate, also a 'system,' won't allow me to talk to my child. She is the gatekeeper to any communication. How can a trained therapist even accept this nonsense?"

And how is it that Rachel, raised in a godly home with devoted, caring parents, ended up falling into these delusions? It was through social media on her cell phone, along with the negative influences of her high school. Her mom simply had no idea what was out there. (How many of us really know what is out there today?) Like many other good parents, she had carefully monitored what Rachel took in as far as movies and TV, and she knew who Rachel's friends were. But she had no idea that Rachel was being indoctrinated and even brainwashed by social media, right through her cell phone, not to mention having these destructive ideologies reinforced by her school.

Tragically, stories like this are not uncommon today. The societal shift has been more dramatic than we realized, and the assault on our children more pronounced than we understood. We must be more vigilant than ever. How many more headlines like this do we need to see? "California Woman, 18, Sues Doctors for Removing Her Breasts When She Was Just Thirteen Because She Thought She Was Trans After Seeing Influencers Online."[24] Our children are under assault.

Back in 1958, after spending four hours of intense interaction and argumentation with Norman Podhoretz, Allen Ginsberg shouted out, "We'll get you through your children."[25] (Podhoretz was a conservative political commentator while Ginsberg, then known as a Beat poet, became an icon in the counterculture revolution of the 1960s, himself a sexual radical and proponent of Eastern religion.)

Ginsberg's words proved prophetic, as the next generation vigorously rejected the values of their parents, discarding the American dream in favor of a supposed new and better way. Then, over time, the young radicals of the '60s and early '70s became part of the mainstream culture, taking jobs in corporate America, in national media, and in the arts and education. Among these former student radicals was Bill Ayers (William Charles Ayers), once a member of the Weather Underground, which the FBI deemed a terrorist group, later to become a distinguished professor at the University of Illinois at Chicago. And although Ayers has personally denied this,[26] others have claimed that he was a mentor to Barack Obama.[27]

As of 2008, Ayers still described himself as "radical, leftist, small-'c' communist,"[28] and regardless of his connection to the former president, there is no denying the influence he had on generations of students he taught. Once again, Ginsberg's words proved prophetic.

In his 1968 White Panther manifesto, John Sinclair, manager of the hard rock group MC5, wrote these shockingly candid words:

> Rock and roll music is the spearhead of our attack because it is so effective and so much fun. We have developed organic high-energy guerrilla bands who are infiltrating the popular culture and destroying millions of minds in the process. With our music and our economic genius we plunder the unsuspecting straight world for money and the means to carry out our program, and revolutionize its children at the same time.[29]

The members of MC5 were young men themselves, yet Sinclair's words echo those of Ginsberg: we will revolutionize your children. And they did. For them, rock was not just loud music. Rock was a revolutionary tool used to change the thinking and actions of young people, contributing to a significant—and for the most part very negative—shift in society.

In July 2006 the UK's National Union of Teachers (NUT) recommended that "it is particularly important to begin to make three- to five-year-olds aware of the range of families that exist in the UK today; families with one mum, one mum and dad, two mums, two dads, grandparents, adoptive parents, guardians etc."[30] Yes, the thinking of the children must be changed, and at the earliest ages possible. Or in the words of a gay drag queen who participated in Drag Queen Story Hours for children, the goal[31] was to "groom" the little ones—not meaning here in a pedophilic, sexual way, although that may have been the goal for some,[32] but in terms of changing their thinking about gays and sexuality.

Sadly, I could multiply examples like this by the hundreds and even thousands, also sharing more stories that would break your heart—from moms, dads, grandparents, and young people themselves. But enough has been said. What can we do in response?

CHAPTER 8

RESPONDING TO THE ASSAULT ON OUR CHILDREN

I F WE ARE to turn the tide in our nation, we must turn the tide with the nation's youth, and this can only be done as we strengthen our marriages and families. Derek Prince once said, "The prevailing attitude toward marriage in any culture or civilisation is usually an accurate barometer revealing its moral and spiritual climate."[1] Quite so. Yet here in America marriage has been unraveling for decades, accelerated by the passing of the disastrous no-fault divorce laws (beginning in California in 1969 under Gov. Ronald Reagan),[2] followed by the radical redefining of marriage by the Supreme Court in 2015.[3] (Reagan later said that signing the bill into law was one of the biggest mistakes he made in his political career.)

Our marriages and homes are under attack, with internet porn becoming a major factor in many a divorce. In fact, a 2011 article published by *Psychology Today* said that "every year for the past decade there have been roughly 1 million divorces in the United States. If half of the people divorcing claim pornography as the culprit, that means there are 500,000 marriages annually that are failing due to pornography."[4] Five years later, in 2016, a headline on the Science.org website stated, "Divorce rates double when people start watching porn."[5] And according to an undated article on the End All Disease website, "Extramarital Infidelity is the leading cause of divorce in the United States. When researchers investigated the effects of porn on marriage, they found that it normalizes the concept of extra-marital affairs, making viewers see cheating as a regular and rewarding thing."[6] And this is just *one aspect* of how marriages are under attack today.

What, then, happens when couples break up (or when kids are born out of wedlock and the dad does not stay around)? What happens to the kids raised in fatherless homes? According to John Stonestreet and Maria Baer,

> one in four American kids are…growing up without their father at home. That amounts to 18.5 million kids.
>
> If statistics hold, this means that 18.5 million children are three times more likely to engage in criminal activity than those who have dads at home. Those 18.5 million kids are more likely to engage in sexual activity earlier, are less likely to go to college, more likely to have emotional and behavioral problems, more likely to struggle academically, are twice as likely to commit suicide, and much more likely to commit violence. The vast majority of mass shooters in the past 20 years were young men who were, in some way, estranged from their fathers.[7]

This is really bad news. But it also points to the solution: solid marriages, led by godly dads and undergirded by godly moms, are God's organic solution to today's youth crisis, not to mention the foundation of a Jesus-centered moral and cultural awakening, and there are decades of statistics to prove it.

GODLY DADS ARE MAKING AN IMPACT

In her 2023 book *The Toxic War on Masculinity: How Christianity Reconciles the Sexes*, professor Nancy Pearcey summarizes the results of a number of studies that surveyed men who professed to be Protestant evangelicals, contrasting the devout from the nominal. On average, Pearcey noted, men who attend church at least three times a month "are more loving to their wives and more emotionally engaged with their children than any other group in America. They are least likely to divorce and they have the *lowest* levels of domestic abuse and violence....Research has found that evangelical Protestant men who attend church regularly are the least likely of any group in America to commit domestic violence."[8] What do you know!

In contrast, nominal Christian men, on average, "spend less time with their children, either in discipline or in shared activities. Their wives report significantly lower levels of happiness. And their marriages are far less stable. Whereas active evangelical men are 35 percent *less* likely to divorce than secular men, nominals are 20 percent *more* likely to divorce than secular men."[9]

And then, "the real stunner: whereas committed churchgoing couples report the lowest rate of violence of any group (2.8 percent), nominals report the *highest* rate of any group (7.2 percent)—even higher than secular couples." (Pearcey suggests that this is because "many nominal men hang around the fringes of the Christian world just enough to hear the *language* of leadership and submission but not enough to learn the biblical *meaning* of those terms" hence the higher levels of abuse and divorce.)[10] As stated by researcher Brad Wilcox, "when you look at measures of paternal involvement, things like reading to your children, volunteering for a Boy Scouts group, coaching sports and so on, active conservative Protestant or evangelical fathers are the most involved fathers of any major religious group in the United States."[11]

Wilcox wrote this in 2004, but numerous studies since then have come to similar conclusions,[12] including studies that have surveyed evangelical Christians in other parts of the world.[13] Along with this, there are the examples that so many of us can point to personally, where kids have been raised in godly (but not perfect!) homes, and those kids are now young adults, also burning bright for the Lord, and in some cases now having kids of their own.

This is not rocket science. If you spend more quality time with your kids and set a good example, you will see far better results, on average, than you would see if you had spent less quality time with your kids and/or set a bad example. As the saying goes, "you teach what you know, but you reproduce who you are." In that sense the apple doesn't fall very far from the tree.

FOUR ESSENTIAL STRATEGIES

Here are four things we must do if we want to see a lasting, gospel-based, moral and cultural revolution. First, we must develop a *multigenerational mentality*. Second, we must become more *fully aware*—and therefore vigilant— when it comes to the war on our kids. Third, in light of that heightened awareness, we must become more *focused and intentional* when it comes to nurturing, raising up, educating, and discipling our children. Fourth, we must recognize the importance of *immersion and encounter*, meaning we must understand how important it is for our kids to get immersed in gospel truths and reality as well as to encounter the Lord for themselves.

1. **Developing a multigenerational mentality.** Traditional Judaism is grounded in this way of thinking, with each generation looking back to the teachings and values of previous generations while also looking forward to imparting those teachings and values to future generations. In fact, some of the most foundational rituals of Judaism, such as the celebration of the Passover, are done as remembrances:

> Obey these instructions as a lasting ordinance for you and your descendants. When you enter the land that the LORD will give you as he promised, observe this ceremony. And when your children ask you, "What does this ceremony mean to you?" then tell them, "It is the Passover sacrifice to the LORD, who passed over the houses of the Israelites in Egypt and spared our homes when he struck down the Egyptians."
>
> —EXODUS 12:24–27

I've written about the importance of having this multigenerational mentality at some length elsewhere,[14] so I'll simply summarize some key points here: 1) We must avoid the danger of thinking we're the last generation, because of which we don't need to think about what kind of world our kids or grandkids (or great-grandkids) will inherit. As much as we *should* live with urgency and long to see the

Lord's return, it is the height of irresponsibility to give little or no thought to what is coming after us. That is the opposite of being good and responsible stewards. 2) Given the fact that many were raised with the teaching that "Jesus is coming any moment," we need to make a holy effort to renew our minds and change our thinking (regardless of our end-time beliefs). Do we give any thought to how the world might look in twenty-five or fifty or one hundred years? As leaders of churches or schools or businesses, do we think of our works outliving us, even thriving and growing after our departure? 3) What are we doing to see that our values and beliefs are being transmitted effectively to the generations that follow us, beginning with those in our home (or directly under our spheres of influence in other settings)?

These two passages are foundational to the thinking of traditional Jews, and they help explain why traditional Judaism has done such a good job of replicating itself over the centuries:

> Hear, O Israel: The LORD our God, the LORD is one. Love the LORD your God with all your heart and with all your soul and with all your strength. These commandments that I give you today are to be on your hearts. Impress them on your children. Talk about them when you sit at home and when you walk along the road, when you lie down and when you get up. Tie them as symbols on your hands and bind them on your foreheads. Write them on the doorframes of your houses and on your gates.
>
> —DEUTERONOMY 6:4–9

(We'll return to that passage shortly.)

My people, hear my teaching; listen to the words of my mouth. I will open my mouth with a parable; I will utter hidden things, things from of old—things we have heard and known, things our ancestors have told us. We will not hide them from their descendants; we will tell the next generation the praiseworthy deeds of the LORD, his power, and the wonders he has done. He decreed statutes for Jacob and established the law in Israel, which he commanded our ancestors to teach their children, so the next generation would know them, even the children yet to be born, and they in turn would tell their children.

—PSALM 78:1–6

2. Becoming more fully aware. As a result of the COVID shutdown, many parents learned more about what their kids were learning in school, since the classes were conducted online and the parents were often right there along with their children. Many of them were shocked, exclaiming, "*This* is what they're teaching my kids at school?" Yet in many cases this was the same material that was being used in those same schools for years, if not decades. The parents simply had no idea, and the children either didn't realize the radical nature of what they were learning or didn't think of sharing it with their parents.

Headlines such as this might seem shocking— "Minnesota's New 'LGBT Education Specialist' Thinks Teachers Should 'Explain Nonbinary Identities' to Preschoolers"[15]—but they are really nothing new at all. In fact, more than fifteen years ago I was told by one of my ministry school students that she had to quit her job as a preschool teacher. That's because she was required to read to the children such books as *Heather Has Two Mommies*,[16] which she could not do in good conscience. And she was not allowed to address the children as "boys" or "girls," since that would be making a gender distinction. Instead, she had to use terms like "friends." This too is madness, yet it was the prevailing philosophy of a highly rated preschool in Charlotte, North Carolina, more than fifteen years ago.

And the bombardment really is coming from every angle, be it TV or movies or comic books or social media or peers. Or do you really think that headlines like this are exceptional and out of the ordinary? "DC Comics Pushes Gay Pride on Children With Same-Sex Superhero Couple 'Midnighter and Apollo.'"[17] And of course there's an accompanying cartoon image of these two men kissing—but really now, that's old hat. Even a book like *King and King*, published twenty years ago and targeting kindergarten-aged kids, featured a same-sex kiss.[18]

What then can we do? Parenting is challenging enough, even in the best of circumstances. (All the more is this true for single parents.) And many parents find it hard to keep their heads above water with so many pressures and responsibilities and commitments. But this is not a battle we can avoid. This is not a conflict we can simply observe from the sidelines. We do not get to sit this one out, and the cold, hard truth is that *our children's lives are on the line, not to mention their very souls.* Do we plead ignorant or say, "Sorry, but I was too busy"?

Somehow we must get more involved in our kids' lives and do an even more vigilant job of standing guard over their hearts and minds and ears and eyes. If your kids are in public schools, it's imperative that you find out what textbooks are being used, what ideologies the schools are pushing, and what curriculum is being taught. And in all cases, wherever your kids are being educated, it's essential that you know what entertainment they're enjoying, from music to movies to TV shows to internet videos, as well as how they're engaging in social media and who their friends are. After all, you're the parents!

And wherever possible, recognizing that you cannot shelter them from everything, do your best to engage them in healthy conversations, to explain why certain things are good and others are bad, and to let them know that you're not threatened by their questions and perspectives. If any place should feel safe for children, it should be their own homes—especially if they're struggling with doubts or grappling with their sexuality or feeling pulled by the desires of the flesh. May we increase our vigilance!

3. Sharpening our focus to teach and train. Now, with our increased vigilance, we must pour truth into our kids, be more involved with them in a positive way (aside from simply trying to protect them from bad influences), prioritize spending quality time with them, and—along with having lots of fun together—do our best to disciple our children. If we don't do it, the world certainly will.

This is obviously a big subject, and I am not an expert in the teaching and training of children. (For decades I have poured myself into young people from college age into their twenties and thirties; I have not specialized in teaching, training, or discipling younger children.) But this much I can say with certainty: 1) our children will follow our example more than our words, 2) they can tell the difference between what is authentic and what is fake, and 3) doing life together is a major key to successful child-rearing.

Along with these general thoughts, let me recommend here these helpful resources:

- Focus on the Family provides a wide range of resources for parents and educators.[19]

- Many excellent books offer guidelines and support to help parents raise godly children in today's challenging environment.[20]

- Numerous practical resources target the church's ministry to Gen Z.[21]

- There are also many helpful resources for homeschoolers.[22]

4. Focusing on immersion and encounter. We read these words from Deuteronomy 6:4–9 a few pages back. Moses spoke them to the nation of Israel before entering the Promised Land:

> Hear, O Israel: The LORD our God, the LORD is one. Love the LORD your God with all your heart and with all your soul and with all your strength. These commandments that I give you today are to be on your hearts. Impress them on your children. Talk about them when you sit at home and when you walk along the road, when you lie down and when you get up. Tie them as symbols on your hands and bind them on your foreheads. Write them on the doorframes of your houses and on your gates.

Traditional Jews take these commandments quite literally, not only in terms of literal phylacteries (small boxes that contain passages from the Torah attached to a man's left arm and forehead during certain prayer times in the day) and mezuzahs (small cylinders placed on the upper right side of every door in a Jewish home, also containing some biblical passages). They also make it their business to talk about God and Torah and religious studies day and night, impressing them on their children in the most immersive ways possible. As for the Hebrew word translated "immerse," it can either come from a root meaning "to engrave"—hence, to cause the words to penetrate your children's hearts and minds (others translate the verb as "teach diligently")—or a root meaning "to repeat," explaining the rendering of the NLT: "Repeat them again and again to your children." This is exactly what traditional Jews do!

I was speaking to a Jewish man from Israel a few months ago who had been raised in an ultra-Orthodox home in Israel. Though he had recently come to faith in Yeshua now that he was in his thirties, he was in every way a brand-new believer. When I asked him what his daily schedule was while in religious high school, he told me they started their day around 7:30 a.m. and ended close to midnight. What a schedule! They would pray and study together in large groups, in small groups, and independently, but all in a very structured way. This was the norm for him. In fact, he had just started going to a ministry school to get immersed in the things of the Lord, but he didn't know what to do with all his free time since classes (including chapel) were only from 8 a.m. until noon daily, and the outside reading and ministry requirements were quite minimal for him. "Why," he wondered, "did we have such lightweight schedules?"

He had just purchased a new car and had to drive across several states with his vehicle. While driving, he listened to the entire New Testament in Hebrew, and when we met together, he could talk about lots of specific details of the text from memory—and this was just after hearing it once. But why not? He had immediately immersed himself in the New Testament just as he had immersed himself in rabbinic texts for years. This, for him, was a way of life.

Am I suggesting that we too keep our kids in Christian schools from early morning to midnight? (In the Jewish setting they lived together in dorms.) Certainly not. But I am saying this: Our kids are already getting bombarded and influenced by social media and video games and binge-watching of TV series, not to mention drugs or alcohol or sex. We should not imagine that a little dab of the gospel here and there will counteract this bombardment. We too must be much more immersive with our kids and the gospel.[23]

This was reinforced to me by Ron Luce, well known in the past for launching the Teen Mania missions movement that positively impacted many thousands of young people. But as he saw the growing needs of the church and the degree to which young people were dropping out, he realized that here in the States a different strategy was needed. He now says that churches should especially focus on sharing the gospel with kids around thirteen years old, and once they come to faith, they should be put in an intensive spiritual immersion program. This, he says, became clear to him after observing the methodologies of rapidly growing churches worldwide, all of which had in common a powerful movement among teens and youth.

Ron and his team have put together a curriculum that churches can follow over the course of several years, broken down into semesters each year, so individual congregations do not have to reinvent the wheel. Ron and his team have already done the heavy lifting. The local church just needs to implement the strategy. Those churches that do, according to Ron, will see these young people grow and remain committed for years to come. In fact, he told me, they will become the next generation of leaders.[24]

The reality is that there is a pitched battle for the souls of our children. If we don't fight fire with fire, we will lose many of our own. It's that simple. If we want to see major breakthroughs and wonderful, lasting fruit, we will have to change our mindset. Half-hearted efforts and once-a-week gatherings will not do the trick. Our kids need to be immersed, and as moms and dads and spiritual leaders we must lead the way.

You might say, "Just reading this overwhelms me. I'm tired enough as it is. Who can think about this type of spiritual immersion?"

I would say in reply that once again I'm not here to condemn, and I'm not your judge. I'm just telling the truth. We are losing way too many of our kids as they grow up, and plenty of others are barely lukewarm. Unless we do something very different, we will not see different results. In the words of Paul in Galatians 4:16, "Have I now become your enemy by telling you the truth?"

A key factor in all this is that our kids must have their own encounter with God. They must know the Lord for themselves and experience Him for themselves. Once they do, it will become much harder for the world to pull them away. This should be a major emphasis of our prayers and our efforts as parents and ministry leaders. How can we help them come to know the Lord for themselves?

In the early 2000s I became aware of a ministry led by the Kirk family in England, basically a mom with her grown son and daughter.[25] They specialized in ministering to children and youth, bringing these kids together for days at a time and teaching them the ways of the Spirit, then, with supervision, releasing them to minister to others. It was astounding to see how these kids were touched and how God used them to touch others. And in the process they became strongly grounded disciples. How we need more of this in our church cultures today.

It's surprising to see how deeply children can be touched by the Lord. It's amazing to see just how profoundly they can come to know Him and trust Him. May the Lord give us His wisdom, His grace, His favor, His anointing, and His strategies to raise up Jesus-loving children who will lead the way in blessing America in the decades ahead.

THE FUTURE BELONGS TO THE CHILDREN (AND THOSE WHO INVEST MOST IN THE CHILDREN)

Did you ever hear the story about the man who owned two dogs that constantly fought with each other? A friend asked him, "Which dog wins when they fight?" He answered, "The one that I feed." It's the same with our kids: they will win the battles they face in their lives if they are properly fed.

Having said that, here's a closing thought. On July 1, 2023, eccentric billionaire Elon Musk tweeted, "The childless have little stake in the future."[26] Who are the "childless" of today? In chapter 7 I discussed the importance of bringing more children into the world, but in many nations the sustainable birth rate has declined dramatically, meaning that future generations will not have the support system needed as they grow older, leading to a national collapse. Consequently, for years now "in rapidly aging Japan, more diapers are used by older, incontinent people than by babies."[27] This speaks of a serious crisis—and similar crises are growing in country after country, from Russia to Spain and from Singapore to Italy.[28]

To break this down, on average, women during their childbearing years (most commonly from eighteen to forty-four) need to have 2.1 children to sustain a society. When the number drops below this, as the country ages, there are not enough children in the workplace to support the older generation (without undercutting their own ability to survive), nor is there adequate family support for the elderly. Unless the trend is rapidly reversed, a point of no return is crossed. It is a dreadful scenario. As Elon Musk, the world's wealthiest man, said at a forum in Italy in December 2023, "it's important to have children and create the new generation. As simple as it sounds, if people do not have children there is no new generation."[29]

But I bring this up here for a reason. It is becoming increasingly common for couples not to have children until they are in their late thirties or early forties. That means on average they will have fewer kids than those who start younger. And more and more couples will have no children at all, by choice. Who then is thinking more about children and the future, the couples with kids or the couples without kids?

In 2017, writing for the Gatestone Institute, which focuses on international public policy, Giulio Meotti stated,

> Europe's most important leaders are all childless: German Chancellor Angela Merkel, Dutch Prime Minister Mark Rutte and the French presidential hopeful Emmanuel Macron. The list continues with

Swedish Prime Minister Stefan Löfven, Luxembourg's Prime Minister Xavier Bettel and Scottish First Minister Nicola Sturgeon.

As Europe's leaders have no children, they seem to have no reason to worry about the future of their continent. German philosopher Rüdiger Safranski wrote: "for the childless, thinking in terms of the generations to come loses relevance. Therefore, they behave more and more as if they were the last and see themselves as standing at the end of the chain."[30]

All of us who have the heart of the Lord, whether or not we have kids of our own, should have a heart for the coming generations. We are pro-life, we believe in the sanctity of marriage, we affirm that children are a gift from the Lord, and we worship a God who identified Himself in the Old Testament as "the God of Abraham, Isaac, and Jacob"—the God of multiple generations! Let us then write the next chapter of our national history by writing it on the hearts and minds of our kids. On with the revolution!

CHAPTER 9

BECOMING THE SALT AND LIGHT OF THE EDUCATIONAL SYSTEM

DID YOU KNOW that 106 of the first 108 colleges and universities in America were founded as Christian schools, including Harvard, Princeton, and Yale?[1] Did you know that their first goal was to train a literate clergy and then to help the general public, based on biblical principles and Christian morals?[2] Did you know that the Bible was regularly used as a textbook in our children's schools until the beginning of the twentieth century?[3] And did you know that one reason some of the colonies wanted to see children learn to read was so they could study the Scriptures for themselves?[4]

To be sure, America is a much more diverse country today, and we do not have enforced Christian laws, as some of the colonies did. More importantly, as followers of Jesus living in America, our goal is not to take over the educational system and force everyone to be educated as Christians—let alone to live as Christians. Absolutely not. But there is no question that the pendulum has swung in a totally opposite, extremely radical, and very dangerous direction, and it is imperative that we regain our positions of influence in the educational systems of America. This is ground we must take back if we want to see a real cultural awakening. As lesbian journalist and author Patricia Nell Warren said in 1995, "whoever captures the kids owns the future."[5]

In my 2022 book *The Silencing of the Lambs: The Ominous Rise of Cancel Culture and How We Can Overcome It*, I shared some shocking data from our universities, writing:

> It is difficult to describe how far our college and university campuses have lurched to the left in recent decades. Suffice it to say that "according to a recent [2018] study on faculty party affiliation by the National Association of Scholars, the ratio of Democrats to Republicans at Williams College is 132:1; at Swarthmore it is 120:1; and at Bryn Mawr it is 72:0. At many of America's best research universities, the ratios are only moderately better." For good reason the 2018 article citing this study was titled "The Disappearing Conservative Professor."[6] How did this happen, right in front of our eyes?
>
> In 2020, a report that focused on Harvard University found the same situation prevailing on that iconic campus: "A recent survey by the *Harvard Crimson* found that conservatives make up just over 1% of the school's faculty."[7] Chew on that one for a moment. The implications are massive.[8]

Then, in January 2023, I wrote this:

> How do we explain the increasing radicalization of our country? How do we explain the decided shift left?
>
> Writing in the year 2000, Roger Kimball noted: "The Age of Aquarius did not end when the last electric guitar was unplugged at Woodstock. It lives on in our values and habits, in our tastes, pleasures,

and aspirations. It lives on especially in our educational and cultural institutions, and in the degraded pop culture that permeates our lives like a corrosive fog....Although sometimes tempted to ignore it, we are living in the aftermath of a momentous social and moral assault."

Kimball's book was aptly titled *The Long March: How the Cultural Revolution of the 1960s Changed America.* It followed his 1990 book, *Tenured Radicals: How Politics Has Corrupted Our Higher Education,* meaning that, by 1990, professors with radical leftist ideas had already become tenured. How far has this corruptive process gone?[9]

The answer is that it has gone much further than we know! In fact, things have shifted so dramatically that Russell Jacoby, a now retired longtime leftist history professor from UCLA who once mocked conservatives for "their nightmare of radical scholars destroying America," now realizes he had things entirely wrong.

Speaking of the generation of the 1960s, he writes:

> In pose we were much more radical than previous American intellectuals. We were the leftists, Maoists, Marxists, Third Worldists, anarchists, and protesters who regularly shut down the university in the name of the war in Vietnam or free speech or racial equality. Yet for all our university bashing, unlike earlier intellectuals, we never exited the campus. We settled in. We became graduate students, assistant professors and finally—a few of us— leading figures in academic disciplines.

He continues:

> Within 30 years, the timber and tone of faculties
> were refashioned. In the 1950s the number of public
> leftists teaching in American universities could be
> counted on two hands. By the 1980s, they filled air-
> planes and hotel conference rooms. In the 1980s a
> three-volume survey of the new Marxist scholarship
> appeared (*The Left Academy: Marxist Scholarship
> on American Campuses, vol. 1–3*). Endless new
> journals, each with their own followings, popped
> up, such as *Studies on the Left, Radical Teacher,
> Radical America, Insurgent Sociologist, Radical
> Economists*. In the coming years leaders of the main
> scholarly organizations like the Modern Language
> Association or American Sociological Association
> elected self-professed leftists.[10]

Worst of all, this destructive reconfiguring of our educational system has made its way down to our children's
schools, even our preschools, and not just in the last few
years. This radical shift has been taking place for decades.
Already in the mid-1990s conservative leaders could speak
of pornographic movies, both heterosexual and homosexual, being viewed in sex-ed classes for high school students. Ten years later, in 2005, GLSEN (the Gay, Lesbian,
Straight Education Network) could announce that "nearly
3,000 schools have GSA's [Gay Student Alliances] or other
student clubs that deal with LGBT issues. Over fifty national
education and social justice organizations, including the
National Education Association (NEA) have joined GLSEN
in its work to create safe schools for our nation's children
through projects like 'No Name-Calling Week.'"[11]

Reading between the lines, what this actually means is that children could be encouraged to "come out" as gay or lesbian to their fellow students and teachers and counselors without their parents ever finding out, and that impressionable kids, from kindergarten on up, would read about famous gays in American history, learn the meaning of terms like *genderqueer*, and discover whether they might be boys trapped in girls' bodies (or the reverse). I own some of the lesson plans used by GLSEN back then. Not a word I'm saying is exaggerated.

That's why it's no surprise that by 2007 the *New York Times* could do a positive story on the Park Day School in Oakland, California, where "teachers are taught a gender-neutral vocabulary and are urged to line up students by sneaker color rather than by gender. 'We are careful not to create a situation where students are being boxed in,' said Tom Little, the school's director."[12]

Is it any wonder that the Daily Caller could report on July 20, 2023, that

> Brown University's student newspaper completed a study concluding that 38% of students at the school identify as LGBT.
>
> The *Brown Daily Herald*, Brown's student newspaper, reported massive increases in the number of LGBT students on campus since 2010. Some of these statistics include a 26% increase in gay/lesbian students, a 232% increase in bisexual students and a 793% increase in the number of students identifying as any sect of the LGBT community, the *Herald* reports.
>
> Overall, these statistics show that the number of LGBT students on campus has tripled in the past

13 years, which is an increase of over five times the national rate.[13]

Be assured that these extraordinary statistics are not the result of something these kids are eating or drinking (there's nothing strange in the water at Brown!). No, this is the result of decades of systematic indoctrination in the schools, coupled with the sociological contagion spurred by social media and Hollywood, mixed in with some typical youthful rebellion against the status quo.[14] That's why a 2021 survey conducted by the CDC found that 25 percent of high school students identified as LGBTQ.[15]

Speaking of sociological contagion, a UK study in 2022 found that ten years earlier "there were just under 250 referrals, most of them boys, to the Gender Identity Development Service"; in other words, there were just under 250 kids who were confused about their gender identity and contacted this national service for help. By 2021 "there were more than 5,000, which was twice the number in the previous year. And the largest group, about two-thirds, now consisted of 'birth-registered females first presenting in adolescence with gender-related distress', the report said."[16] How, pray tell, did this happen? And should I mention that 2022 was the year that UK Health Services *shut down* the now infamous Tavistock clinic in lieu of claims of medical malpractice?[17]

THE INFILTRATION HAS BEEN SYSTEMATIC AND INTENTIONAL

About fifteen years ago I was speaking with a Christian woman whose doctorate was in educational administration and whose job gave her a bird's-eye view of what was happening in schools from K-12. She told me even then that for many years there had been a disproportionate gay presence among teachers and administrators in the schools, quite visible every year at the annual gathering of the National Education Association (NEA).

Rather than this being a secret agenda, the NEA has been quite open and proud about it, with a special "Toolkit" of "NEA LGBTQ+ Resources," announcing, "This resource page is designed to provide educators with LGBTQ+ information, tools, and resources they need to support transgender and non-binary students, to be more inclusive of LGBTQ+ history in their classrooms, and to stop LGBTQ+ bias and intolerance in our public schools."[18] So this is not simply a matter of reducing bullying (that can best be done by teaching that all bullying is bad). It is a matter of indoctrination, as link after link on this site makes clear.

More broadly, articles have been written on "The Marxist Takeover of American Institutions," noting how radical academics in the 1960s "aimed to achieve long-term social and political change by infiltrating and subverting key institutions, particularly the elite universities they often attended."[19] (This echoes what professor Jacoby wrote, as quoted earlier.) What a great job they did! Another article explained:

> First, radical leftist beliefs and values have gained more and more influence in our universities year after year. It is hard to get exact numbers on the viewpoints wittingly or unwittingly promoted by professors, but notice the significant decline in the number of conservatives that teach in universities in the USA.
>
> 1969—Approximately 1 in 4 were conservatives
> 1999—Approximately 1 in 10 were conservatives
> 2019—Approximately 1 in 17 were conservatives

That was where things started. And then?

Secondly, the influences on the left are moving further to the left, into a witting or unwitting Marxist worldview (and away from true, freedom-promoting liberalism). Starting about twenty years ago, Critical Theory was introduced more and more into the soft sciences in universities (humanities like history and psychology) and then, in the last ten years, it has moved into the hard sciences (math, engineering, etc.) and now into all fields. It now is the dominant philosophy.[20]

It is for good reason that law professor Jonathan Turley tweeted on June 1, 2023, "Nationally, less than a third of American[s] identify as 'liberal' but Harvard and other schools show over 75% [of] professors identify as liberal. That does not happen randomly. It takes a consistent culture of intolerance for opposing viewpoints."[21] Yes, these radical changes did not occur randomly. They are the result of a decades-long, systematically planned takeover of our schools from the ground up (and from the top down).

And what happens when conservatives try to break in on the college and university level as professors and scholars? Turley notes, "The trend is the result of hiring systems where conservative or libertarian scholars are often rejected as simply 'insufficiently intellectually rigorous' or 'not interesting' in their scholarship. This can clearly be true with individual candidates but the wholesale reduction of such scholars shows a more systemic problem. Faculty insist that there is no bias against conservatives, but the falling number of conservative faculty speaks for itself."[22] The bias is real, undeniable, and well-documented.[23]

As noted in a March 2, 2021, article in the *Free Beacon,* "Research from the Center for the Study of Partnership and Ideology released Monday shows that conservative professors and graduate students are 'guaranteed' to face discrimination in academia. University of London politics professor Eric Kaufmann conducted the study, which he says is the first to focus on how academic authoritarianism threatens conservatives on campus." Worse still, "Kaufmann told the *Free Beacon* that the trend is likely to get worse. Twenty percent of academics under 30 support 'dismissing' peers deemed controversial, Kaufmann said. Thirty percent of doctoral students say they would discriminate against grant bids from right-leaning researchers or decline to promote a conservative peer."[24]

This also means that many of those conservative academics who do have university positions choose to self-censor to preserve their livelihoods. Consequently, while the radical leftists dominate the campuses and speak openly and freely, the conservatives represent a small minority and often do not speak up at all.[25] No wonder so many of our students are so deeply confused.

As summarized by Christopher Rufo,

> today, America's cultural revolution has reached the endgame. The descendants of the New Left have completed their long march through the institutions and installed their ideas into school curricula, popular media, government policy, and corporate human resources programs. Their core set of principles, first formulated in the radical pamphlets of the Weather Underground and the Black Liberation Army, has been sanitized and adapted into the official ideology

of America's elite institutions, from the Ivy Leagues to the boardrooms of Walmart, Disney, Verizon, American Express, and Bank of America.

As a result,

> the critical theories of 1968 have turned into a sub-stitute morality: racism is elevated into the highest principle; society is divided into a crude moral binary of "racist" and "anti-racist"; and a new bureaucratic logic is required to adjudicate guilt and redistribute wealth, power, and privilege. To enforce this new orthodoxy, left-wing activists have established departments of "diversity, equity, and inclusion" across an entire stratum of the public and private bureaucracies. Allies are rewarded with status, position, and employment. Dissenters are shamed, marginalized, and sent into moral exile.[26]

This is where we stand today. What must we do to turn the tide?

THE LONG MARCH BACK

Let's state the obvious first: if there was a long march to bring about this negative transformation, it would likely take a long march to undo this damage and create better learning environments for children and young adults. Are we up to the task? Or do we really have a choice? The good news is that every step in the right direction makes a tangible difference and affects real lives, just as when someone who is one hundred pounds overweight loses two pounds a week. Every day that person has become healthier than the day before and has taken another step toward their goal. It's little by little, but it's all in the right direction.

There's also good news in that we already have thousands of Christian schools across America, along with Christian colleges and universities and ministry schools and seminaries, not to mention an army of homeschooling families. So to the extent these institutions stay true to God and His Word, they can play a major role in the rising gospel-based counterculture revolution.

In my book *Saving a Sick America: A Prescription for Moral and Cultural Transformation*, I laid out this agenda for turning the tide in our educational system:

> How then do we address the massive problems in this critically important part of our society? The solution is simple and doable, although daunting in scope: (1) we confront the spirit of relativism with absolute truth and morality; (2) we learn to reengage our own minds, and we teach our kids to think; (3) we get more involved in children's education, becoming school teachers and administrators and librarians and counselors and local school board members (or at least, meet with our kids' teachers and be aware of what's happening in their schools); (4) we prioritize raising up more Christian schools and developing more homeschooling networks; (5) we get more involved in higher education, becoming professors and administrators at secular colleges and universities; (6) we develop more Christian alternatives for undergraduate and graduate studies with the end goal of either influencing current accreditation institutes (which often lean left) or rendering them unimportant.
>
> And this is where we start: we engage *our minds*

in serious study of the Scriptures. In doing so, we will be stretched, we will be challenged, we will grow, and we will learn to love God with our hearts and minds. Then we teach our kids to do the same.[27]

Here I'll focus on four key strategies.

First, we must keep cultivating the homeschool revolution. When the modern homeschool movement began in the 1970s, it really was quite revolutionary. Who had heard of such a thing? Sending your kids to a religious school was nothing new. But the idea of keeping them home, with parents (mainly the mothers) teaching their kids, seemed quite strange, if not downright dangerous. Wouldn't this rob them of a quality education? Would this hurt them in terms of socialization? And what about academic standards and protocols? How would they be enforced?

According to a January 2023 article on the How Do I Homeschool? website, homeschooling is currently illegal or restricted in Germany, Sweden, Norway (for children under age twelve), Austria (for children over age fifteen), Greece, France, Finland, Spain, Belgium, Italy, Portugal, Czech Republic, Slovenia, Slovakia, Hungary, Romania, Bulgaria, Croatia, Cyprus, and Malta.[28]

Homeschooling remains controversial in many highly developed parts of the world. Here in America there was a state-by-state battle to legalize homeschooling, and in 1983 the Homeschool Legal Defense Association was formed "to defend and advance the constitutional right of parents to direct the upbringing and education of their children and to protect family freedoms."[29]

In the early years of the movement kids would graduate from their home high school, only to find it difficult, if not impossible, to get into many colleges in America. Their work was not taken seriously, and their grades and accomplishments were downplayed or disregarded. (Some of this is understandable, given the lack of evenness that existed in the movement; some of it was simply biased and discriminatory.)[30]

And in those early years, the number of families involved was small. Today, there are "about 3.1 million homeschool students in 2021–2022 in grades K-12 in the United States (roughly 6% of school-age children). There were about 2.5 million homeschool students in spring 2019 (or 3% to 4% of school-age children). The homeschool population had been growing at an estimated 2% to 8% per annum over the past several years, but it grew drastically from 2019–2020 to 2020–2021."[31] (A 2021 article puts the number even higher, estimating that between four and five million American kids are now homeschooled, representing 8–9 percent of school-aged children.[32])

Of course, not everyone who homeschools shares our biblically based beliefs, but homeschooling gives the parents the ability to take control of their children's education. They can establish the environment in the home. They can be intimately involved in the curriculum. They can guarantee that their kids get more time with them than with nonbelieving (and in some cases very worldly) teachers and peers. They can keep all unwanted influences out. (No one is going to be handing out condoms to middle schoolers in their home!)

Not every family is called to homeschool, and many others are simply not able to do it. But for those that are, they don't need to do it on their own. There are all kinds of support networks, both in person and online, along with numerous resources and curricula. And, in keeping with an emphasis in the previous chapter, this allows for a much more immersive learning experience.

A 2021 article in *Psychology Today* noted (with caveats because of limited research) that "homeschooled students tend to score higher on tests of academic skills when compared to children in public schools across most studies." In addition, "most studies find that homeschooled children tend to have higher college GPAs than children from conventional schools." As for social skills, some seemed to do better than kids from public schools, and others worse.[33]

More importantly, what would a study look like comparing the spiritual commitment of Christian kids who were homeschooled with Christian kids who went to public schools? I'm not aware of such a study, but it would not surprise me at all if the results were dramatically in favor of the kids taught at home. On many levels homeschooling provides a better environment for discipling and nurturing. And as this movement continues to grow, involving a higher and higher percentage of our children, the national impact could be truly revolutionary—*but only if we put in the necessary effort and time.*

That's why it is so important for local churches along with national denominations to find ways to undergird their homeschooling families. This truly is a key to turning the tide.

Second, we must strengthen our Christian schools, colleges, and universities. These schools are some of our greatest assets, places where kids and young adults can be trained and equipped, environments in which they can be grounded in a biblical worldview and given a vision to make a positive impact on this world. But there is the caveat: *they must be truly Christian.* They cannot compromise their beliefs or morals for the sake of accreditation or funding or popularity. If they do, they lose their effectiveness, becoming like the salt that lost its saltiness. Of what good is it? (See Matthew 5:13.)

Often, though, these schools, especially K–12, are underfunded and consequently understaffed. This adds an unnecessary strain to the already challenging task of teaching and training kids from a wide range of Christian backgrounds (some schools accept non-Christian students too), making it more difficult to provide the highest-quality education. That's why here too churches in local communities should work together to support these schools, while Christian businesses and businesspeople should do their best to help finance them as well. And whether the financial support is there or not, Christian educators, from teachers and administrators to librarians and coaches, should ask the Lord if He wants them to serve in the Christian school sphere.

The fact is that many families are not able to home-school their children, while others feel that professional educators are better qualified to teach their kids academically. Either way, these schools provide an important alternative to the public school system and have the potential to raise up a generation of godly revolutionaries. And the more funding they have, the more they can offer scholarships for needy children, the more they can offer transportation, the more they can have viable sports programs, the more they can provide state-of-the-art technology, and the more they can do things with excellence.

But again, the key is that they remain Christian in the truest and fullest sense of the word. Their goal is not to become like the world or to demonstrate their "wokeness" or to show how "balanced" they are or to keep the radical leftist educators satisfied. Their whole calling is to be countercultural, wherever the culture has departed from the ways of God. That's why I say they have the potential, along with homeschooling families, to raise up a generation of godly revolutionaries. We must fight fire (the fire of an often godless educational system) with fire (the fire of biblically based education).

That's why it is also critical for the schools to be backed by parents, churches, and Christian legal foundations when they are challenged for staying true to their standards. For example, one of the finest and biggest K–12 Christian schools I know of went through a multiyear attack because it expelled a student who was an open and practicing homosexual. Had the student been an unrepentant, heterosexual fornicator who was expelled, there would have been very little backlash.

On the college and university level, the greatest challenge is to refuse to compromise, whether it is due to pressure from accreditation associations, pressure from the government or courts, pressure from more "progressive" students or faculty, or pressure from the world—in other words, the pressure to not appear fanatical and extreme.

A seminary professor told me about thirty years ago that the time might come when their national accrediting association would require them to change their views on homosexuality. He told me quite matter-of-factly that should that day come, their choice was obvious: they would stay with the Word. After all, as Jesus asked, "What good will it be for someone to gain the whole world, yet forfeit their soul? Or what can anyone give in exchange for their soul?" (Matt. 16:26).

Sadly, other schools yielded to the pressure—in the

name of doing what was best for their students. This happened to Trinity Western University in Canada, the nation's largest Christian university, after the Supreme Court of Canada ruled that Trinity could not operate its law school unless it changed its Christian charter, which the court considered discriminatory against LGBTQ+ students. As a Christian university, the school had covenantal standards that both faculty and students were required to live by, with one of those forbidding homosexual relationships even though they were legal in Canada.

After years of court battles and back-and-forth rulings, the Supreme Court ruled against the school 7-2. If their law school was to be recognized by the Canadian Bar Association, the standards would have to change. In response to this, I wrote an article on June 16, 2018, that ended with these words:

> Honestly, I don't know where TWU goes from here. And I don't know how the believers in Canada will respond.
>
> But I can say this to my friends and colleagues and fellow-educators and communicators here in America: We either use our liberties or lose them. We either stand fast and stand tall and stand strong, or we cower in a corner. We either do what's right today, or we apologize to our children tomorrow.
>
> It's time to push back.
>
> What will you do?[34]

I can tell you what Trinity did, sadly. They removed the Christian covenantal standards, issuing this statement: "In furtherance of our desire to maintain TWU as a thriving community of Christian believers that is inclusive of all students wishing to learn from a Christian viewpoint and underlying philosophy, the Community Covenant will no longer be mandatory as of the 2018–19 academic year with respect to admission of students to, or continuation of students at, the University."[35]

I'm sure there was tremendous pressure on the school, and the leadership certainly wanted to be able to train and equip Christian lawyers. The battle had been long and exhausting, and now the school had come to the end of the road. Wouldn't it be better to relax their regulations to have a law school—a Christian law school!—rather than hold fast to their community standards and have no school at all? Not in God's sight. Better to honor Him and keep the standards high, coveting His blessing more than anything, than to bow down to the ungodly pressure of the world to save their school. To paraphrase Jesus here, "If you save your school, you lose it. If you lose your school for Me and the gospel, you find it" (based on Mark 8:35).

Other Christian colleges and universities have compromised in other ways for other reasons. In the end this will result in them losing their saltiness as well. Who needs a semi-Christian college or university? In contrast, schools like Liberty University or ORU that largely continue to hold to biblical standards, without compromise or apology, will be blessed and thrive. (A professor at Liberty told me a few years ago that they were now training about 50 percent of future military chaplains. What kind of difference will this make over the course of a generation?)

My exhortation is clear and direct: Christian schools and colleges and universities, hold fast! We need you standing strong and standing tall. As one university chancellor recently said in a letter to the parents of prospective students, you have spent your whole lives raising your kids to be godly. Don't send them someplace where all this training will be undone. You can trust your kids with us! (This is a paraphrase of his words.)

Really now, if some of our most prominent universities can be so unabashedly anti-Christian, if they can proudly promote the extreme (and even bizarre) ideologies, and if they can be proud as they do all this, why on earth should we who have the words of life and the wisdom of God dilute our doctrines or compromise our convictions? For what purpose? To what end? To please whom?

Let us be truly biblical. Let us be authentically Christian. And let us be revolutionary—in the holiest, godliest sense of the word.

Third, we must regain our influence in the public school system, from preschools to university campuses—in some cases even regaining the leadership. This, again, is a "long march" strategy, but if the world could do this without the help and anointing and wisdom of the Lord, surely we can with His help and anointing and wisdom. It is part and parcel of our multigenerational thinking.

Some might say, "But we are to come out of the world, so all our emphasis should be put on Christian schools and institutions."

I would reply, "We are to come out of the world in terms of sin. We are to go *into* the world in terms of winning the lost and shining the light and making a positive impact. Otherwise, how can we function as salt and light in the world if we are not intimately involved with the affairs of this world?"

That means God will call some of us to be first-grade teachers just as clearly as He calls some to be missionaries.

And both callings will be equally sacred and important. The same can be said for the calling to be school librarians or administrators or professors or chancellors. If we look at these positions the way we look at the calling to the mission field—sacred in God's sight and with a clear gospel purpose—we can better take hold of our vocational mission in the school system.

Christian academics can even lead the way in many key fields, just as the sciences were once led by Christians. As for the leaders of our universities, did you know that until 1967—meaning just two years before Woodstock—all the presidents of Boston University were Methodist ministers?[36] And did you know that from its founding in 1701 until 1899 all the presidents of Yale were also ministers, from Rev. Abraham Pierson (1701–1707) until Rev. Timothy Dwight (1886–1899)?[37] Those were obviously different days from today, but if such radical, left-leaning changes could take place in the last two generations without God's help, why can't radically positive changes take place *with* His help?

Consider that the president of the American Library Association, Emily Drabinski, is a self-professed "Marxist lesbian" who said publicly, "The consequences of decades of unchecked climate change, class war, white supremacy, and imperialism have led us here. If we want a world that includes public goods like the library, we must organize our collective power and wield it." She added, "The American Library Association offers us a set of tools that can harness our energies and build those capacities....I will direct resources and opportunities to a diverse cross section of the association and advance a public agenda that puts organizing for justice at the center of library work."[38] That sounds like quite an agenda. Libraries certainly do have power to shape and influence the thinking of children.

That's why it's not enough for us simply to be present in the public school system. We must make an impact. That means teachers and administrators and librarians and counselors and principals and professors and presidents and chancellors must put obedience to God before personal security and safety. (I'll have more to say about this later in the book when I make reference to what one tenured professor calls "kamikaze academics.")

It means that some of us, when told we must do something that violates our conscience (such as refer to a boy as "she"), must say with respect and humility, "I'm sorry, but I cannot do what you're asking me to do. It is against my faith, and it violates my constitutional rights." At that point, local believers and leaders need to surround that courageous person with prayer and support, while Christian legal foundations call on the school to do what is right. And what happens if it means a protracted court case? What happens if it means getting threats online? What happens if it hurts our career, at least in the short haul?

I'll answer these very real, very weighty questions with questions of my own. What happens if none of us takes a stand? What happens to the children? What happens to the next generation? And how will we look our persecuted, even martyred, brothers and sisters in the eye when they share their stories of suffering for the faith?

One of my ministry school grads working in the Muslim world told me that before they baptize a former Muslim, they ask them, "Are you willing to die for Jesus?" It's the same with my dear friend Yesupadam in India (I mentioned him in chapter 6). After asking the baptismal candidate if they affirm the fundamentals of the gospel and that Jesus is their Lord, he then asks them, "Are you willing to give your last drop of blood for Jesus, your last breath?" After they say yes, he immerses them in water. Does this answer the questions that were just posed? And has there ever been a revolution of substance that came without a cost?

During the time I was writing this chapter (but unknown to her), Nancy sent me a meme to post online. It was a simple black-and-white picture of a little child, with the caption "They're not after you, they're after me! You need to be in the way."

To all those in the public school system, I ask you: Are you willing to be in the way?

Fourth, we must expose the folly and extremism of the current educational system while also invading the schools with the gospel. This means parents need to speak up at school board meetings as well as schedule private meetings with teachers and administrators as needed. (In the next chapter we'll talk about running for school board positions.) We must expose the craziness of the curriculum; we must push back against the Marxist agenda; we must shout to the world that the emperor's new clothes are no clothes at all. Many are waking up these days, but we cannot take our foot off the gas. This is also how we stand "in the way" of those whose agendas for our kids are very different from our own.

In addition to this, there are ways we can bring the gospel right into the schools without violating any laws or infringing on the rights of others. I know of some churches that are doing this very effectively.

One of them, New Life Church, based in Corpus Christi, Texas, works with kids wanting to start Bible clubs in their schools. These clubs normally meet after hours, with a Christian supervisor helping out, and of course it's all voluntary. And no matter what some public school leaders might say, it's totally legal and protected by the law. As of this writing, New Life works with Bible clubs in twenty local schools, including elementary, middle, and high schools. What a wonderful harvest field! They're also seeing great results on the local university campus, regularly doing outdoor baptisms under a big fountain on the grounds.

The pastor of New Life, Mike Felhauer, told me, "Each Bible club requires a teacher sponsor, and the clubs must be student led. At least one youth leader is allowed to be present at each Bible club, and between our paid youth staff and volunteers we have one youth leader at every Bible club. The students, though, lead the groups—calls for salvations, prayer for healing, and so on. Some even have additional teachers showing up to be ministered to."[39] What a wonderful kingdom investment!

Pastor Mike sent me a series of pictures showing the growth in just one of the clubs. It started in a classroom. It now meets in a gym. The harvest is very ripe!

The fact is there will always be Christian kids in the public school system. Some of them are there because the school environment is fairly positive; others are there because their parents don't want them sheltered from the pressures of the real world; others are there as missionaries and evangelists; others are there because there are no Christian schools in the area or because the cost is too high; others are there because homeschooling is not an option for their family. If we can help these Christian kids get organized, give them guidance in their approach and goals, and equip them to build up other believers in the school as well as reach the lost, we can see amazing results.

What if we, as parents of kids in the public school system, encouraged them to start Bible clubs, finding a sympathetic faculty adviser who could be involved? And what if other churches, like New Life, could say, "We will get behind this as well, investing our staff in the club." The harvest is ripe, and we have the answer to the deepest problems of life.

As for these very real problems, they are so pronounced in some school districts that principals and administrators have reached out to local churches for help. "We don't know what to do," these school leaders are saying, "and we are at our wits' end. The depression, the drug use, the suicides, the promiscuity, the violence—it's too much! Can you help?"

Help can take many forms, including (a real example from twenty years ago) a class in a local high school that was devoted exclusively to teen moms and pregnant teens.

I work closely with one church that has received such calls for help, and they have sent out students from their leadership school. Here's a report I received on August 1, 2023. It will encourage your heart! (I left out the name and location of both the school and the church for privacy's sake.)

> For the last year and a half, we have been invited into a local public middle school. This school was rated one of the worst in the state. Many of the families represented at this school are either involved in drug/human trafficking or incarcerated. Some kids are homeless, many of the teachers deal with fights in the school and classrooms multiple times a week.
>
> The principal invited students from the leadership school into the lunch periods for building

relationship and discipleship for the 7th and 8th graders. We have seen over 100 students give their lives to Jesus just during lunch. We have also seen healings and miracles break out. One kid that came to lunch with crutches no longer needed them after he received prayer.

At the lunches we invite the students to our Bible club that [we] host at the school after school on Fridays. At the Bible club we have seen kids saved, filled with the Holy Spirit and set free....

At the close of the Bible club this year we held baptisms offsite at a nearby church parking lot. Also, since we have gotten involved in the school we have seen many of our church members and leadership school students become faculty members at the school. We are just getting started because this upcoming year we have a second middle school opening up its doors to us. We are expectant that God is moving in power to radically save this generation.[40]

What a wonderful report! And all this is happening at a public school.

But isn't it high time for this to be happening? When mandatory assemblies are held in which kids are indoctrinated with the most radical LGBTQ+ activist ideas, when some of these assemblies also include "gay Christian" kids telling the others that God is OK with homosexuality (a concerned mother once called my show with this very story), and when students are penalized or even expelled for refusal to comply, how can we *not* walk through every open door that is set before us?

And as long as school officials open the doors, we have every legal right to walk through. The more kids in these schools are transformed, the less we will hear people shouting, "Separation of church and state!" The fruit will speak for itself.

Let us do all this for the sake of the children, our most sacred entrustment from the Lord. We really can do no other. So on with it! This is an essential part of our gospel revolution.

While working on this section of the book, I was in Tübingen, Germany, for a series of meetings with some dear friends based there. A young man in the congregation named Florian Kubsch approached me. Years earlier he had driven me around when I was in Germany. He presented me with a book he had written titled *Crossing Boundaries in Early Modern England: Translation of Thomas à Kempis's "De Imitatione Christi" (1500–1700)*. The book is based on his doctoral dissertation, and although Florian is German, it is written in excellent English. He also held in his hand a copy of my 2022 book *The Political Seduction of the Church*, in which I also spoke of our need to get more involved in the education system.

In the front of the book, he wrote this to me: "Dr. Brown—You were a great inspiration for me to pursue my PhD and, thus, 'position myself more deeply…in education' [quoting from *Political Seduction*]. Thank you for your great example of wisdom and being on fire for God!" He is now teaching at a high school in his city, following God's calling on his life to be salt and light in that public school system. May the Lord multiply men and women like Dr. Florian Kubsch around the globe!

CHAPTER 10

CHANGING LAWS AND CHANGING HEARTS

BILL BRIGHT (1921–2003) is best known as the founder of Campus Crusade for Christ, one of the largest campus outreach ministries in the world; author of the famous *Four Spiritual Laws* evangelism booklet; and producer of the *Jesus* film, which has been viewed more than *eleven billion times* in over two thousand different languages, making it one of the most significant evangelistic projects in history.[1]

But Dr. Bright was not just a visionary evangelist who founded Campus Crusade (known today as Cru). He was also the founder of the Alliance Defending Freedom (ADF), America's "largest legal organization committed to protecting religious freedom, free speech, marriage and family, parental rights, and the sanctity of life."[2] That's because he understood that protecting our foundational American freedoms went hand in hand with our ability to preach the gospel without restriction. As Bright said, "I truly believe we are fighting for the very survival of the gospel and of evangelism in America today."[3] (Bear in mind that he passed away in 2003; even then the assault on our liberties was very real.)

Since 2011 the ADF has been directly involved in fifteen major Supreme Court wins, most notably *Dobbs v. Jackson*

Women's Health Organization in June 2022, which led directly to the overturning of *Roe v. Wade*. It doesn't get any bigger than that! Other cases of note that were successfully litigated by the ADF before the Supreme Court include *303 Creative v. Elenis* (2023), which was a major victory for Christian freedom of conscience and expression; *Uzuegbunam v. Preczewski* (2021), on behalf of a Christian student who was blocked from openly sharing his faith on his college campus; and *March for Life Education and Defense Fund v. California* (2020), stating that employers did not have to "provide their employees with abortion-inducing drugs, sterilization, and contraception—regardless of their religious or moral convictions."[4] Had these cases, among many others, been decided differently, our country would look very different than it does today.

Another major Christian legal organization is Liberty Counsel, founded by attorney Mathew Staver. Liberty Counsel has also been involved in major Supreme Court victories, some of them helping to preserve critically important aspects of our religious freedoms. To cite one case in point, on May 2, 2022, Liberty Counsel announced,

> Today, the U.S. Supreme Court ruled 9-0 that the City of Boston violated the Constitution by censoring a private flag in a public forum open to "all applicants" merely because the application referred to it as a "Christian flag." The High Court stated that it is not government speech, and because the government admitted it censored the flag because it was referred to as a Christian flag on the application, the censorship was viewpoint discrimination, and there is no Establishment Clause defense.[5]

The ruling was so obvious and the anti-Christian discrimination so blatant that the court ruled 9-0 in favor of the Christian client. Yet without groups like Liberty Counsel litigating these cases, the discrimination might have continued and even increased. Other fine Christian-based legal organizations include the ACLJ, founded by attorney Jay Sekulow, as well as the Pacific Justice Institute, Becket, and the Rutherford Institute, among others. We owe a massive debt to these fine organizations, which are helping make America a better place for all citizens.

This points to the importance of Christian legal work since without it not only could our essential rights and freedoms be removed, but we could be compelled by the government to say or do things contrary to our faith, resulting in loss of job, expulsion from colleges and universities, steep fines, and even prison sentences if we refused to comply. Even worse, our children could be taken from us and put into state care (foster homes) if we refused to act and speak as the government demanded. In fact, as I write this in the summer of 2023, California is considering a law that would remove children from the homes of parents who refuse to affirm their child's perceived gender identity.[6] This is outrageous beyond words, but it's exactly where things could be heading without Christian legal organizations pushing back and without Christian voters electing representatives who will push back against these godless laws in the halls of Congress, and other elected officials who will appoint righteous judges to the courts.

Tragically, at this very moment there are at least twenty-two states in America where *it is illegal* for minors to receive professional counseling to help them deal with unwanted same-sex attractions or unwanted gender identity confusion.[7] Illegal! Even if they had been sexually abused as children, even if their parents supported them fully in their choices, even if the request to see a counselor was entirely their own without any outside coercion, it is now illegal in all these locations for minors to receive these essential services. In fact, in 2018 California came close to passing a bill that would make it illegal for any person of any age to receive such counseling.[8] This is absolutely chilling.

In stark contrast, a ten-year-old boy can be put on dangerous puberty-blocking hormones (that would likely sterilize him for life, not to mention potentially lead to other significant health risks), and a thirteen-year-old girl can have her breasts removed simply because these children are going through a time of gender-identity confusion. And all this is perfectly legal. Talk about calling good evil and evil good. Talk about legislating unrighteous behavior and criminalizing righteous behavior.

That's why it is so important that we keep fighting for our freedoms of conscience, speech, and religion—in the courts and in the voting booths. If we don't, it will not be long before pastors will be told what they can and cannot say from the pulpit, Christian schools will be told what portions of the Bible they can affirm and what parts they must denounce, and homeschooling Christian parents will have their kids taken from their care, should they teach anything deemed unacceptable by the state.

Not a word of this is alarmist or exaggerated in the least, as can be easily documented. In fact, some of the very things I have just listed *have already taken place* in other countries, while there have been attempts to make this the law here in America.[9] And for several years there has been a pitched battle on a national level as to whether girls can be forced to share bathrooms and locker rooms with boys who identify as girls (including having to change in their presence), not to mention be forced to compete against them in sports. (Both the Obama and Biden administrations have pushed for these policies aggressively, based on so-called "transgender rights.") The battle is very real.

On a positive note, since the overturning of *Roe* in June 2022, numerous pro-life bills have been passed, and the momentum continues to grow.[10] As reported by Jordan Boyd for The Federalist in May 2023, "Less than a year after the Dobbs v. Jackson decision, half of U.S. states proudly have laws protecting life in the womb between conception and 12 weeks." She added, "In the last two months alone, Republican legislators and governors in more than half a dozen states enacted laws that save the lives of tens of thousands of unborn babies."[11] This is excellent news. Innocent lives *are* being saved.

Not only so, but for the first time in its forty-year history, the Human Rights Campaign (HRC), the world's largest LGBTQ+ activist organization, declared a state of emergency in June 2023 (for some of the larger context see chapter 4.) The HRC proclaimed,

> We have officially declared a state of emergency for LGBTQ+ people in the United States for the first time following an unprecedented and dangerous spike in anti-LGBTQ+ legislative assaults sweeping state houses this year.
>
> More than 75 anti-LGBTQ+ bills have been signed into law this year alone, more than doubling last year's number, which was previously the worst

year on record. Our community is in danger, but we won't stop fighting back—not now, not ever.[12]

I take no pleasure in seeing these fellow Americans upset, feeling that *their* rights are under attack. But for the most part I believe these legislative efforts are good and righteous pushing back against a destructive LGBTQ+ activism that in the end does far more harm than good. This too is very positive news, and it is imperative—I cannot say this any more clearly—that we continue with these legislative efforts, from the local courts to the halls of Congress and from the desks of governors to the desks of the president. Even a quick study of the Scriptures indicates how important it is to God that righteous laws be put in place.[13]

WE MUST CHANGE HEARTS ALSO

Even more important than laws is that we seek to change hearts and minds. Put another way, we must win in the court of public appeal as well as in courthouses throughout the land. We must change the thinking of millions of Americans lest the legislative victories of one generation get swallowed up with massive reversals in the next generation, if not even more quickly. What a terrible shame that would be.

Thinking back to the eradication of slavery in the 1700s–1800s, how was it that William Wilberforce (1759–1833) and the abolitionists in the United Kingdom and America succeeded in their mission? Slavery was a way of life, with national economies built on its very back. There was no way political leaders would even think of outlawing the practice—unless their own eyes and the eyes of the people could be opened to the horrors of slavery.

To give just one example of how deeply entrenched the slave trade was in British life, John Newton (1725–1807), author of the world-famous hymn "Amazing Grace," continued for a few years as the captain of a slave trading ship *after* his radical conversion experience. As he explained (to his shame) years later, "Custom, example, and interest had blinded my eyes. I did it ignorantly."[14] In other words, slave trading was the common practice of the day (custom); everyone he knew, including Christians, had no real problem with it (example); and it was profitable (interest).

That's why Wilberforce—a parliamentarian fighting on a governmental, as well as popular, level—and his colleagues launched graphic PR campaigns using the image of a chained African man asking, "Am I not a man and a brother?" They also utilized the testimonies of former slaves (and even former slave traders, like Newton), ultimately changing the law by changing public opinion. It was in that same spirit that President Abraham Lincoln allegedly said to Harriet Beecher Stowe (1811–1896), author of the watershed novel *Uncle Tom's Cabin*, "So you're the little woman who wrote the book that made this great war!"[15] He was speaking, of course, of the Civil War. Whether the quote is true or not, Stowe's book was greatly used to change the thinking of millions of Americans. They came to realize that the African slave trade was downright evil. It had no business in our country at all.

That's why the changing of hearts must accompany the changing of laws. Otherwise, there will ultimately be resentment, anger, and rebellion, leading to the reversal of the good laws we fought so hard to pass. The short-term gains will become long-term losses.

Earlier in the book we looked at some of the effective

strategies used by LGBTQ+ activists, but I want to focus here on one of their most successful strategies in changing American hearts and minds. These activists, who were committed to fighting legislative battles, recognized that the greater battle was for hearts and minds. The changing of laws would follow suit.

I was reminded of this when reading some old reviews of the watershed 1989 gay activist book *After the Ball: How America Will Conquer Its Fear and Hatred of Gays in the 90's*, by Marshall Kirk, a neuropsychologist, and Hunter Madsen, an advertising executive. While the book's importance has often been downplayed by gay leaders over the decades, its influence is undeniable. *After the Ball* was a best seller in its day (Who was reading it if not for largely gay-identified Americans?), and it was reviewed in significant outlets such as the *Los Angeles Times*. The reviewer there noted:

> One out of 10 Americans is gay, according to Marshall Kirk and Hunter Madsen in "After the Ball," and these 25 million men and women are "forced to cower and skulk like a German Jew of the '30s." They are the victims of "a national sickness" that manifests itself in the fear and hatred of homosexuality. The only appropriate response from the gay community—and the only way to put an end to their oppression—is "ice-cold, controlled, directed rage."
>
> But "After the Ball" is not a call to the barricades; rather, it is a curious call to the story boards and 30-second spots of Madison Avenue, a kind of sanitized upscale media radicalism that finds mass demonstrations to be "ghastly freak shows" and prefers highway billboards that "earnestly propound appealing truisms, the safer and more platitudinous,

the better." As the authors readily admit: "We're talking about propaganda."[16]

And that propaganda worked wonders, just as the authors envisioned.

A review in the *Orlando Sentinel* had this to say: "'Some gays, living in their progressive urban environments, think America is tolerant and there is no need to build greater public support. They feel the way now is only through the courts and the legislatures,' says Madsen. 'They are all good tactics, but they are reversible, as soon as someone— usually on the religious right—fans the flames of public disapproval.'"[17]

To go beyond the courts and legislatures then, since those rulings could be reversed, it was necessary to change perceptions. Accordingly, the authors' goal was the "conversion of the average American's emotions, mind, and will, through a planned psychological attack, in the form of propaganda fed to the nation via the media." As stated earlier, Kirk and Madsen called for a "campaign of unabashed propaganda, firmly grounded in long-established principles of psychology and advertising."[18]

This propaganda even included the spreading of what they knew to be falsehoods, such as the idea that one in ten Americans was gay (they admitted this number was inflated). But in their view, spreading such falsehoods was only fair since all kinds of negative falsehoods had been spread about their community over the years. As to the success of their strategies, which reflected some of the thinking of other key gay activists and organizations, not even Kirk and Madsen believed that marriage would be redefined. Not a chance. That wasn't even one of their goals.

But that sacred institution was outrageously redefined in 2015 by the Supreme Court largely *because* the thinking of so many Americans had already been changed. Without that massive cultural shift, it is much less likely that the court would have ruled as it did. In the view of many legal pundits, the cultural shift provided sufficient wind in their sails for the justices to make the change (at least for someone like Anthony Kennedy, who was the swing vote).

To be sure, some of the shifts in American views toward gay- and lesbian-identified people have been positive, recognizing the many good qualities they may have as individuals or couples and reminding us of our shared humanity. Many of the other shifts have been disastrous, contributing to millions of Americans losing their moral and societal bearings. Our children and grandchildren are paying the price today, with as many as 40 percent identifying as somewhere on the LGBTQ+ spectrum.[19]

The takeaway from all this is that while we labor tirelessly to enact pro-life, pro-family legislation, we must never take our eyes off the greater prize: conversion of the hearts and minds of Americans by the spreading of truth, grounded in the love, goodness, and justice of God. We have the ultimate, lasting, winning argument.

Did Charles Finney Predict the Civil War?

In chapter 2 I mentioned how God used Charles Finney in the city of Rochester, New York, in 1829–1830. But Finney was not only a powerful evangelist; he was also a strong abolitionist. When he was president of Oberlin College in the years before the Civil War, the school functioned as one of the stops on the Underground Railroad, helping slaves escape to the North.[20] Still, Finney was very clear in his priorities: the gospel must come first, including evangelism and revival; social change must come second. To reverse the process could be deadly. Literally.

That's why in 1835 he wrote a letter to his staunch antislavery colleague, Theodore Weld, who came to faith through Finney's ministry, urging him to reconsider his methods and to put changing of hearts first and the abolition of slavery second. He wrote:

> Br.[other] Weld, is it not true, at least do you not fear it is, that we are in our present course going fast into a civil war? Will not our present movements in abolition result in that?...How can we save our country and affect the speedy abolition of slavery? This is my answer....If abolition can be made an appendage of a general revival of religion, all is well. I fear no other form of carrying this question will save our country or the liberty or soul of the slave....
>
> Abolitionism has drunk up the spirit of some of the most efficient moral men and is fast doing so to the rest, and many of our abolition brethren seem satisfied with nothing less than this. This I have been trying to resist from the beginning as I have all along foreseen that should that take place, the church and world, ecclesiastical and state leaders, will become embroiled in one common infernal squabble that will roll a wave of blood over the land. The causes now operating are, in my view, as certain to lead to this result as a cause is to produce its effect, unless the publick mind can be engrossed with the subject of salvation and make abolition an appendage.[21]

Looking back through the lens of history, Finney's warning was chillingly prophetic, as indeed "ecclesiastical and state leaders" became "embroiled in one common infernal squabble" that rolled "a wave of blood over the land." There is a lesson for us here today.

We must put first things first in terms of our emphasis, our priorities, our efforts, and our hearts. The moment these begin to shift is the moment we become less effective. To the extent our emphasis and priorities and efforts and hearts continue to shift, to that extent we guarantee the short-term nature of our success—if we succeed at all. The inevitable flow of the world will carry the next generation in its tide. The people who have not been won to the Lord or had their minds changed through godly reasoning will become all the more determined to fight back and retake what they've lost. That's why the counterculture revolution must be gospel based. The church must lead the way.

This reminds me of an old video clip from healing evangelist T. L. Osborn (1923–2013). He was talking about official opposition to the preaching of the gospel in Ukraine and said that the government leaders should welcome local and foreign evangelists. And why was that? Because, he said, the government can't make a bad person good. But the gospel can. That's why in all our efforts to change the laws—and these efforts are *crucially important* for the good of the country—we must never take our foot off the pedal of prayer, evangelism, discipleship, and apologetics as we make our case to the nation.

We'll tackle the many different ways we can make our case later in the book, but for now, as we transition to the next chapter, let me share with you another quote from Aleksandr Solzhenitsyn's commencement address at Harvard in 1978. He said, "We have placed too much hope in politics and social reforms, only to find out that we were being deprived of our most precious possession: our spiritual life. It is trampled by the party mob in the East, by the commercial one in the West."[22]

Do we have ears to hear this warning? Do we recognize that our narcissistic, materialistic, self-centered, flesh-gratifying American culture must also be confronted if we are to see lasting change—and that we must change our *ways* as well as our *laws*?

In his 2007 book *God & Government*, Charles Colson (1931–2012) referenced this same speech by Solzhenitsyn, noting that he "listed a litany of woes facing the West: the loss of courage and will, the addiction to comfort, the abuse of freedom, the capitulation of intellectuals to fashionable ideas, the attitude of appeasement with evil." He added,

> Solzhenitsyn lamented that two hundred years ago, as the Constitution was being written, or even fifty years ago, when Walter Lippmann was trying to preserve the husk of Western virtue, it would have seemed quite impossible...that an individual be granted boundless freedom with no purpose, simply for the satisfaction of his whims....The West has finally achieved the rights of man, and even to excess, but man's sense of responsibility to God and society has grown dimmer and dimmer.[23]

To recover lost legislative ground then, we must also recover lost ideological ground, reminding Americans that our "unalienable" rights—and our dignity and purpose as human beings—are tied to our being created in the image of God. If we want to see good, lasting fruit, we must re-lay solid foundations, addressing the causes of our problems rather than the symptoms of our problems. If we fix the roots, we fix the fruits.

CHAPTER 11

POLITICAL ENGAGEMENT WITHOUT POLITICAL SEDUCTION

HERE IN AMERICA we live in a democratic republic whose Constitution begins with the words "We the people." That means if we don't like the current government, we can change it. We can vote people out and we can vote people in, and the people we vote for are expected to do our bidding. They can remove bad laws and institute good laws, all at our direction. And if they fail to do what they promised to do as our public servants, we can elect someone who will, or we can run for office ourselves. That's the beauty of living in a democracy.

But there's also a great responsibility on us as Christian citizens of America, since if we don't vote regularly and wisely, others with very different agendas *will* vote. And so just as our presence in the voting booth (and beyond) makes a massive difference, so also our absence in the voting booth (and beyond) makes a massive difference.

Unfortunately, when it comes to Christian involvement in politics in America, we tend to go to one extreme or the other. Either we drop out entirely (for any number of reasons, including pessimism, indifference, fear of getting polluted by the world, or simply the notion that this world is not our home), or we confuse politics with the gospel, looking to human beings or political parties to do what only the gospel can do and becoming as carnal and divided as the world.

In 2022 I published *The Political Seduction of the Church: How Millions of Americans Confused Politics With the Gospel*. I don't believe many of us have learned the lessons from the 2020 elections, and I am deeply concerned about the state of the church as we enter the intensity of the next election season.

Will we be deeply seduced again? Will we wrap the gospel in the American flag? Will we look to a human being to "save" America? Will we become an appendage to a political party? Will we become better known as followers of a political leader than followers of Jesus? Will we attack each other over our support (or rejection) of a particular candidate? Will we expend more time and energy and finances over the elections than over prayer, evangelism, discipleship, and acts of compassion? Will we get so caught up in election fever that we lose our communion with God? Will we focus more on prophecies about the elections than on prophetic words calling us to get our own spiritual houses in order? All of these remain valid questions and concerns.

But this is only one side of the equation. As my dear friend James Robison said to me when interviewing me on his TV show about *The Political Seduction of the Church*, "Michael, I believe the greatest seduction of all is when the church drops out of politics entirely." This is very true!

Some Christians think the world will only get worse before Jesus comes. Why then should we bother to vote? It's all going downhill from here! (This can be a self-fulfilling prophecy since if we don't vote, things *will* get worse.) Other Christians have lost faith in the political system since the people we vote for constantly let us down. Why bother to vote and lobby and campaign and donate? For what? In the end it's just one big political game. For others it's a matter of compromise since the political world seems so corrupt and fleshly. How can we participate in this? For others it's a matter of perspective: "We are not of this world. We are from above, not below. Politics is of this world; it's not for us." Others believe that Jesus is coming any minute, so why bother with elections or make plans for the future? For still others it's simply a matter of indifference. Other things have their attention, things that are more pressing and, to their minds, more relevant. As for the elections, who cares about that? (Or alternately, "Other Christians focus on politics. I'll leave the voting to them.")

The fact is that if we want to see lasting societal change, we must get involved in politics, each according to our calling. For some it will simply mean being informed voters. For others it will mean preparing voter guides to inform those voters. Some will be called to lobby, others to run for office, and still others to write and lecture on political topics. Some will be tasked primarily with prayer (although they should vote too). Others will help underwrite candidates and fund campaigns (of course, they will vote as well). But all of us, one way or another, should be involved.

At the same time, it is critical that we get involved in a right spirit, not looking to politics to do what only the gospel can do. Politics can change laws; the gospel can change hearts.

That's why I often say that politics is one of the primary ways the church can change America, but it's toward the bottom of that list. Here's my own top seven list on how the church can change the nation, reflecting much of the content of this book:

1. Personal and corporate repentance and turning to God for spiritual renewal

2. Prayer and fasting

3. Evangelism and church planting, with an emphasis on making solid disciples

4. Getting our families healthy and strong, pouring into our marriages and kids

5. Serving the hurting, the poor, and the most vulnerable in our communities

6. Positioning ourselves more deeply within the major sectors of society, from education and business to media and entertainment, demonstrating how God's ways work best

7. Staying politically involved by being informed, voting, and supporting those called to frontline political activity

LET'S THINK ABOUT LOCAL POLITICS FOR A MOMENT

When it comes to our political involvement, most of us think about voting for the president every four years, which is certainly a very important vote—perhaps the most important vote of all. Then, we think about our senators and representatives and governors, then our mayors, then other local officials, if we even think about them at all. But how many of us even bother to think about school boards and city councils? Yet those are the very elected officials that set many of the policies that affect our lives (and our kids' lives) on a daily basis.

Some years ago I joined with colleagues from my home church in making a powerful presentation to the local city council during one of its regular monthly meetings. Ten different people could speak for three minutes on any relevant issue, from a request to put in a new traffic light to a complaint about noise in the neighborhood to a concern about potholes in the road. On this particular night our folks called in several weeks ahead and booked all ten of the speaker spots. Not only that, but we filled the meeting hall that night. (Normally the building was almost empty during these meetings, which were usually quite boring and uneventful.) And all of us addressed the same subject when we spoke: we were concerned about vulgar and inappropriate public displays at the annual gay pride event, which took place in the presence of little children.

One of my colleagues began his talk by saying, "If you agree with my position, please stand." All of us then stood to our feet, leaving a handful of shocked onlookers still sitting in their seats and leaving the city council members visibly stunned. It was a powerful night, we bore powerful witness, and we made our point in a powerful yet Christ-centered way. And what was the result of our efforts? Well, we may have made an impression, but we didn't change any votes. The council was decidedly liberal, and nothing we said was about to change their minds.

We also lobbied the school board over concerns about

LGBTQ+ curriculum, in particular curriculum that blurred (or confused) gender distinctions, warning about where this would lead. And since the school board said they wanted to hear from the public, we instructed our congregants to call the board members directly. Our people were so effective in doing this that one school board member called me after getting my number from our church. He was fairly irate, asking, "Who or what is this FIRE Church?" He had been bombarded by concerned phone calls, and I told him politely that he and others had said they wanted to hear from us directly. They did!

And what were the results of these efforts? What happened when we testified before the school board in person, during a night when any number of people could testify? I actually brought samples of some of the radical curriculum being used in schools across America, holding the material in my hand as I spoke. One of the board members said, "That is not what is in your hands!" He denied the curriculum even existed.

This too was a powerful night, and we raised our voices loudly and clearly. A stranger actually came up to me in a grocery store, thanking me for speaking with sanity. She was a concerned mom who had seen me on the local evening news where a clip from the school board meeting was played. And what was the result of our united efforts? Once again, nothing happened. The board voted according to its political leanings, 6 (liberal) to 3 (conservative), just as we were told in advance. The vote was determined before we even got there, and virtually nothing any of us said that night was going to turn the tide.

From this we learned two big lessons. First, as a politically active friend informed us, unless we were there month in and month out, taking an interest in the larger affairs of the local community, the boards and councils would ignore us. In their minds, we only showed up when we had a special interest of our own, but we didn't seem concerned with the larger public good. Second, if we wanted better outcomes, we needed to replace the bad board members with good ones. It was that simple.

The good news is that more and more believers, especially those who are part of large congregations and can literally bring the numbers, are saying to the school boards, "Since it's clear you have your own agenda and are not concerned with what we have to say, and since your views are not representative of the communities in which we live, we will run for office ourselves." The results have been dramatic, with district after district seeing an overhaul of the school boards.

Of course, critics will say this violates the separation of church and state, with some crying, "Christian nationalism! Dominionism! You're trying to establish a theocracy!" Said another way, "When we impose our radical leftist reeducation program on your children, we're doing a good thing. When you push back against our radical agenda, you're a religious fanatic, trying to impose Christianity on our kids." But of course!

The debate will be intense, for sure.[1] As a December 2021 headline on an ultra-liberal site announced, "Dominionism-Driven Christian Nationalists for School Board."[2] In their view our efforts to "take America back" and "take back the ground" are seen in the worst possible light, as if we want to take dominion over other human beings. We must stay our course regardless of the criticism and exaggerated attacks.

Taking Back Versus Taking Over

Many Christian conservatives in America *do* believe it is their job to "take back" what the devil stole from us here in America. You can count me in that group. I want to reclaim the lives that have been destroyed by porn, demonically inspired social media influencers, destructive school curriculum, and abortion. Absolutely! I want to take this "land" back. I would also be delighted if our movies and TV shows and songs, not to mention our universities and beyond, became less immoral, less anti-Christian, less hostile to freedom of speech. That would be great.

But that will *not* come by imposing Christianity on the nation. That is not our place nor our calling, and it is certainly not the essence of the gospel. We will not "take back ground" by some kind of top-down imposition, other than by advocating for righteous laws to protect the innocent from abuse and harm (to give one example of the types of legislation we should fight for). And so in our schools we are not looking to make Bible reading mandatory (although it would be great for every student to become familiar with the Bible as literature, for many reasons). We are not looking to require all students to join in formal, daily prayer. When I say "we," I mean my friends who are on the front lines of the political and educational wars in America.

At the same time, you better believe we want to get rid of a radical LGBTQ+ curriculum in our schools, to give one of the most prominent examples of the destructive indoctrination of our children. We want to get rid of classes where middle schoolers learn about the use of condoms. We want to get rid of an environment where kids are sent home from school because their Christian-themed T-shirt made a faculty member feel "unsafe" (this faculty member can offend the morals and beliefs of the kids in her class on a daily basis without any recrimination). We want to remove sexually explicit books from the school libraries. We want to revise classes that make our kids feel guilty because they are Americans, especially if they are White Americans. (We want our history taught fairly, however uncomfortable that might make some of us. America has an incredible history and yet a very blemished history. For more on this, see the reference to the BH365 curriculum in chapter 13.)

Looking back at the last few years, although COVID brought much pain—partly because it really was a deadly epidemic, and partly because of some of the decisions made in response to it—COVID also brought some things to the surface: parents found out exactly what their kids were learning since the lessons were now being taught online. Many were shocked to learn how radical some of the curricula was, yet this had been happening right under their noses for years, without them having any idea at all. "Enough is enough," they said. It was time to get involved.

Coupled with this was the left's overplaying of its hand, resulting in some of the pushback I described in chapter 4. The same parents who had no problem with same-sex couples having the right to marry had a big problem with a fifteen-year-old boy sharing the locker room with their fifteen-year-old daughter, not to mention competing against her in sports. "Not on my watch," they said. "That's my child you're messing with!"

In many cases their voices have been ignored, and some of the outraged parents have even been likened to "domestic terrorists" by the Biden administration.[3] But their messages are getting out, and the pushback is accelerating.

This Is All Good News, but...

In winning these victories, we have also suffered some defeats. To the extent we have appeared to be bullies, and to the extent we have relied solely on numbers to bring about change, we have alienated those we are called to reach with the gospel and given a false impression of who Jesus is. And we have added more fuel to the fires of suspicion that as Christians we want to take over the society and impose the Bible on everyone else.

So while we get out the vote to replace radical leftist school board members, let us also do our best to reach out to our political opponents privately. While we stand on line waiting to testify at a local hearing, let us also make every effort to befriend those on the other side of the issues. [Remember that the same Jesus who said, "Blessed are those who hunger and thirst for righteousness, for they will be filled," also said, "Blessed are the peacemakers, for they will be called children of God" (Matt. 5:6, 9)].

It was in this same spirit that I made appointments with local LGBT activists when I first got involved in the culture wars in greater Charlotte almost twenty years ago, having one-on-one meals with some key leaders—not to argue with them but to hear their hearts and show them a human, loving face in the midst of our deep differences. In 2013, when I was having lunch with a young, local gay activist named Matt Comer, himself a professing Christian, he realized that he had misjudged me and apologized for some of his wrong perceptions. With tears running down my face, I said to him, "Matt, I just want you to know the love of the Father." He was visibly shaken.

To my knowledge, Matt remains a committed gay activist.

But whereas he once thought of me as "hateful, deranged, and dangerous," after our lunch he wrote that "I've finally come to see more and more of his own humanity, particularly a more private and sincere side of him I'd never seen before. I'm now convinced that Brown honestly does believe everything that comes out of his mouth." (This was published in his op-ed piece in *QnotesCarolinas*, the gay newspaper for the Carolinas, which he then edited.)[4]

In his mind, of course, this just meant that I was quite deluded, even speaking of my "unique brand of lunacy." (Hey, I don't get this kind of compliment every day!) And he wrote, "I've struggled immensely with my thoughts, opinions and feelings toward Brown, especially in recent weeks. Since his debate on homosexuality with Orthodox Jewish Rabbi Shmuley Boteach in early November, I've often sat alone thinking about my interactions with Brown. I've gone back and read many of his writings, my writings and our interactions. It's hard to despise a man when pity starts to take over."[5]

That's why he titled his editorial "A Prayer for Michael Brown," to which I subsequently replied in my own editorial for *QnotesCarolinas*.[6] Contrast all this with his earlier editorial in which he claimed that I engaged in "a carefully plotted and scripted message of 'compassion,' 'love' and 'gentleness,'" calling it a "disguise." He also called me a "predator" and a "wolf in sheep's clothing," referring to those who agreed with me as "fanatics" and comparing me to a Middle Eastern terrorist. (The editorial was originally accompanied by a ridiculously photoshopped image that depicted me as a Muslim terrorist with an AK-47 in my arms!)[7]

What's most interesting here is that in his words he "often sat alone thinking about" our interactions and that

"I've gone back and read many of his writings, my writings and our interactions." It appears that he could not reconcile my sincerity, my love, and my knowledge with, in his view, my dogmatic, outmoded, harmful, anti-gay convictions. Perhaps in the years ahead the Lord will help him realize that it was not that I was delusional or a lunatic but that I had the heart of God. Perhaps the Lord will grant him repentance too!

Somehow then, in the heat of the culture wars and our frontline involvement in the very messy world of politics, we also must remember this directive from Paul to Timothy: "And the Lord's servant must not be quarrelsome but must be kind to everyone, able to teach, not resentful. Opponents must be gently instructed, in the hope that God will grant them repentance leading them to a knowledge of the truth, and that they will come to their senses and escape from the trap of the devil, who has taken them captive to do his will" (2 Tim. 2:24–26). And we must remember this wise adage from Derek Prince: "What will cause the world to notice the church will not be political power. It will be spiritual power."[8]

THE HIGHER WE GO IN THE WORLD OF POLITICS, THE DIRTIER IT GETS

What happens when we move from local school boards to city councils, and from the city to the state and the nation? With each rung we climb on the ladder, we see things get uglier and dirtier: more money involved, more corruption involved, more power involved. The "good old boys" mentality prevails, and ethics and morality come in a distant second to historic loyalties. The deal-making mindset runs rampant, saying, "I'll scratch your back if you scratch mine." There is an increasing desire to win the favor of people to stay in politics, even at the cost of compromising your ethics and softening your stands. And a flood of despicable, even blatantly false, accusations will come against you and your family if you dare mess with the system or challenge the status quo, in both the Democratic and Republican parties. The mudslinging is unrelenting, and it is very hard not to get dirty.

That's why many fine Christians with the best of intentions either get crushed on their way up the political ladder, never to rise again, or they lose their way, selling their souls for the sake of a vote. Those who sell out may end up with a good political appointment, but they will do nothing good with it. Their convictions are all but gone.

Because of the GOP's pro-life, pro-family, pro-Israel platform, in stark contrast with some of the Democratic platform, I have consistently voted Republican for many years, although I am registered as an Independent for conscience's sake. (I am not affiliated with a party; I vote based on the issues.) It is the same with most of my ministerial colleagues in terms of their own voting preferences. They too vote Republican. Yet two of them recently told me how "evil" the local and state Republican parties were (one lives in the Northeast, and the other in the south Midwest). They could not believe how much corruption they encountered when members of their churches ran for office. And they said this as committed Republican voters, believing that the GOP was far better than the Democratic Party!

To be sure, there are many good people in the world of politics. Not everyone is a sellout. Not everyone is corrupt. Not everyone has lost their way. And our votes do count.

The outcomes of our elections can have massive consequences for decades to come. But at all times we must remember that *we cannot look to politics to do what only the gospel can do.* There are no political saviors, and neither party is righteous in the Lord's sight, let alone functioning as "God's party."

That's why it is essential to keep our foot on the pedal of prayer, revival, evangelism, apologetics, and doing good, even if our preferred candidate becomes president and our preferred party takes over Congress. Those electoral victories could be very positive *if* we continue to do our job on the grassroots, community level, functioning as salt and light, and *if* we continue to be known more as followers of Jesus than as supporters of a political candidate. But if we take our foot off the pedal (which we often do), if we put our trust in the political system to reform America, if our advocacy for a candidate is louder than our devotion to Jesus, in the end those short-term victories could become long-term losses. Our testimony has been soured, our reputation tarnished, and we have put our trust in the arm of flesh. That is always a counsel of despair.

As for those called to run for office, the higher you climb the ladder, the stronger your foundations need to be. The more publicity you get, the cleaner your character needs to be. And the more you grow in power and influence, the closer you need to be to the Lord. If you're called to live and thrive in that world, you'll need prayer support and as strong a team of godly advisers as any prominent pastor or Christian leader—if not more.

For a firsthand, deeply personal account of how challenging it can be for a solid Christian to climb the political ladder, I encourage you to read *Jesus and Politics* by Bunni

Pounds, with endorsements from political leaders such as former vice president Mike Pence and a foreword by James Robison. Bunni has also launched Christians Engaged with the goal of getting Christians involved in politics.[9]

There's one more challenge we need to address—or should I call it a seduction rather than a challenge?

GODLY CHRISTIAN PATRIOTISM VERSUS UNGODLY CHRISTIAN NATIONALISM

On July 23, 2023, I tweeted, "As we get closer to the frenzy and intensity of the coming election season, as patriotic Americans who love the Lord, let us never forget that there is a massive difference between chanting 'Jesus! Jesus!' and shouting 'USA! USA!' Massive."[10] That's because there is a massive difference between the kingdom of God and America. The problem is that as followers of Jesus concerned with the good of our country, we share many of the same goals as our non-Christian (or nominally Christian) fellow citizens.

For example, most conservatives in America, whether they are believers or not, want to see secure borders, reduced government, lower taxes, a strong military, Islamic terrorism defeated, communist China resisted, and support for Israel. Most conservatives would also feel proud to be Americans, and while recognizing our seriously blemished history, they would feel that the good far outweighs the bad. Many would even recognize our largely Christian roots.

At the same time, while we share many of these same goals, we as followers of Jesus cannot join in the "USA!" chants with the same passion as others. That's because we feel the terrible weight of abortion, recognize the depth

159

of our carnality, grieve over exportation of porn, and are ashamed of our country's aggressive LGBTQ+ "pride." So while we are *in* this world, we are not *of* this world, and that means our spirit and attitude and emphasis and vision will often be different from that of the world.

All too often, though, in our desire to see our nation turn back to its many Christian roots, and in our passion to see America saved, we mix the gospel and politics in a very dangerous way, resulting in an unhealthy form of Christian nationalism. To address this error, Dr. Joseph Mattera and I drew up a statement in 2022, part of which said this:

> As for "Christian nationalism," **WE RECOGNIZE** that for some, this simply refers to a healthy form of Christian patriotism, of loving God and loving one's country. In that sense, the term is benign.
>
> **WE ALSO RECOGNIZE** that some media outlets put the worst construction on our words, take us out of context, falsely associate us with dangerous, fringe groups, and unfairly malign us. For those who genuinely want to separate fact from fiction, we make these clarifying statements.
>
> **WE RECOGNIZE** that America has a rich Christian heritage, despite its many historic failings, and that to the extent we have honored that heritage, the nation has been blessed. And we applaud those who encourage other Americans to pattern their lives after Christian principles that have helped bring God's favor to our nation through the generations.
>
> In addition, **WE BELIEVE** that nationalism is a biblical concept in the sense of nations having defined borders and identities, as mentioned by

Paul in Acts 17 and by Moses in Deuteronomy 32. God sets national borders and governments and authority spheres for a purpose.

WE ALSO BELIEVE in the positive value of respecting national borders and national authority, in contrast with an international one-world government.

At the same time, **WE REJECT** as unbiblical the belief that America is a uniquely chosen nation, similar to Old Testament Israel being the chosen nation of God. (Although God has used the USA in various ways to bless the world with humanitarian aid and military support, and although the Church of America has sent out missionaries worldwide, in the New Testament, Jesus, as the King of kings and Lord of lords has a special assignment for every nation, tribe, kindred and tongue represented on the earth.)

WE ALSO RECOGNIZE that there is a dangerous and unhealthy form of "Christian nationalism," one that speaks of a potential Christian uprising against the government or hints at the use of force to advance God's kingdom.

WE CATEGORICALLY AND UNEQUIVO-CALLY DENY any affiliation with or connection to that form of Christian nationalism.

Because **WE BELIEVE** that God made one human race expressed through different ethnicities and races, all of which deserve dignity and respect as His image bearers, **WE REJECT** all ideologies and movements claiming ethnic or racial superiority.

WE DENOUNCE calls to violent, armed resistance in the name of Christian nationalism or as an alleged means of advancing the cause of the gospel.

WE REJECT the triumphalist, top-down, take-over of society as part of a so-called "dominion mandate," also noting that we do not know of any major Christian movement that espouses such a top-down, take-over mentality.

WE REJECT the merging of Christian identity and national identity, as if the Kingdom of God and our particular nation were one and the same.

In contrast, WE BELIEVE the biblical way to influence society is by living the cruciform life in which believers lay down their lives in the service of others, resulting in human flourishing for the glory of God. This can include Christ-like engagement in every sphere of society.

And WE DO BELIEVE that Christians have as much right as any other group to have their voices heard in the public square and to influence society, functioning as the salt of the earth and light of the world, and we encourage such activities as good citizens of our various nations and as part of our sacred calling.

WE BELIEVE that Christians should seek to make a positive impact on every aspect of society, including education and media, along with politics, and that by acting on gospel principles, whole nations can be changed.

WE BELIEVE that Christians should be politically informed, should exercise their right to vote, should hold elected officials accountable, and when called by God, should run for political offices themselves.

BUT WE SEE IT AS SPIRITUALLY DANGEROUS IF/WHEN...

- We wrap the gospel in the American flag (or any national or state flag).

- We equate our country with the Kingdom of God.

- We confuse patriotism with spirituality.

- We compromise our ethics to keep our party (or leader) in power.

- Our church/denomination/ministry becomes an appendage of a political party.

- We put more trust in earthly methods than in spiritual methods.

- We marry the cause of Christ to the cause of a political party (or leader) as if they were one and the same.

- We become as vulgar and rude as the candidates we follow.

- We look to the White House or any branch of government in any nation more than to God.

- We make a human being into a political savior.

- We equate loyalty to God (which should be unconditional) with loyalty to a party or political leader (which should be conditional).

- Our prayers and our prophecies become politically partisan.

FINALLY, WE CONCLUDE BY CONTRASTING THE KINGDOM OF GOD WITH EXTREME NATIONALISM:

- The *Kingdom of God* prioritizes the advancement of the gospel. *Extreme nationalism* prioritizes the advancement of its ideology even at the expense of the gospel.

- The *Kingdom of God* produces loyalty to Christ above all else. *Extreme nationalism* produces loyalty to one's nation above all else.
- The *Kingdom of God* raises the banner of Jesus above all else. *Extreme nationalism* raises the national flag above all else.
- The *Kingdom of God* promotes the interests of God above the world. *Extreme nationalism* promotes the interests of one's nation above the Kingdom.
- The *Kingdom of God* views the world through a biblical lens. *Extreme nationalism* views the world solely through a geopolitical lens.
- The *Kingdom of God* is dependent upon neither an earthly kingdom nor an earthly ruler but upon Jesus as the King of kings (Revelation 19:16). *Extreme nationalism* is dependent upon both the ideology of an earthly nation and its ruler.
- Followers of the *Kingdom of God* are passionate about a Christ-centered global awakening. Adherents of *extreme nationalism* are focused primarily on a political/ideological awakening.
- *Christ-followers* are primarily identified with the Kingdom of God. *Extreme nationalists* derive their primary identity from their nation.
- *Christ-followers* derive their primary value from being children of their heavenly Father (Romans 8:14–17). *Extreme nationalists* derive their primary value from being citizens of their country.

May the Church put God's Kingdom and His righteousness *first* so that He can trust true believers, who genuinely represent His heart, to be the salt of the earth and the light of the world.[11]

Can we simply opt out of politics? Absolutely not. We must be involved for the good of the nation today and the sake of the next generation tomorrow. The key is to be involved the right way with the right spirit, the right priorities, and the right emphasis. If we do this, in force, activating our base to get out the vote, America will be the better for it.

For the last twenty-five years, our church has held an annual missions conference in October, raising support for the many missionaries we have helped send out around the world, most of them graduates from our ministry school. It is a highlight of the year for our community and a very sacred time.

A few years ago, as we were singing a worship song about the harvest of souls worldwide, I was overcome with my love for the people of the nations. (I have ministered outside the United States on roughly 200 trips, more than 160 of them overseas. My heart beats deeply for the nations.) I fell to my knees, weeping, and said, "Lord, I will give myself to go to the nations with the gospel! I will gladly devote the rest of my life to missions!" At that moment the thought came to mind, "Then why am I so involved in advocating for a gospel-based moral and cultural revolution here in America?" Immediately I heard the response: "As America goes, the world goes."

This underscores why it is so important that 1) we stay involved in the political battle here in America, and 2) we do so in the right spirit. It is not just about our country. It is about the rest of the world.

Someone once said that politics is downstream from culture. I would add that culture is downstream from the church—at least when the church of a nation makes up a substantial part of that country. And when it comes to America, the nations are downstream from us. Let us take this sacred stewardship seriously.

CHAPTER 12

FOLLOW THE MONEY TRAIL

HAVE YOU EVER heard of Larry Fink? What about a company named BlackRock? Until recently, both Fink and BlackRock were completely unknown to me and, I would imagine, to the vast majority of Americans. Yet behind the scenes Fink and BlackRock were making an enormous impact on our culture, directing *trillions* of dollars into different companies and doing so with the clear agenda of changing the behaviors and values of those companies. If you want our money, they were saying, you'll do things our way.

Fink is the CEO of the BlackRock investment firm, and many Americans were shocked when an interview he did in 2017 came to light in 2023. Without apology—to the contrary, with a clear sense of moral imperative—Fink said in the video, "Behaviors are gonna have to change and this is one thing we're asking companies. You have to force behaviors, and at BlackRock we are forcing behaviors....If you don't force behaviors, whether it's gender or race or just any way you want to say the composition of your team, you're gonna be impacted and that's not just not recruiting. It is development."[1]

So BlackRock would use the massively powerful leverage of trillions of dollars to *force the behavior of companies*. Does this help explain the increasingly illogical, pro-trans business decisions made by companies such as Target and Anheuser-Busch?[2]

One of my colleagues, who is well-read in many fields and circumspect in his comments, wrote to me privately, saying, "The big pressure that Larry Fink can now exert with money is amazing. BlackRock is so vast and powerful (Should this power be legal?) that they can rate companies and downgrade them for not supporting ESG-DEI [environmental, social, and governance; diversity, equity, and inclusion] standards and so not recommend them. So the downstream CEO's of companies conform and go to work to not be on the bad side of BlackRock. Fink may be one of the most dangerous men in U.S. history."[3]

Paraphrase: You do things our way, or else. We intend to force your behavior.

The Daily Wire reported on June 20, 2023 that "independent journalist James O'Keefe dropped a bombshell video on BlackRock Inc.—a prominent investment management and financial services firm—revealing just how broad the company's impact might be.

"A journalist working for the O'Keefe Media Group (OMG) spoke with BlackRock recruiter Serge Varlay—who told her that because of the vast sums of money the company controls in the global market, they can essentially 'run the world.' He began with a caveat, noting that BlackRock did not necessarily want people to notice what they were doing."[4]

O'Keefe actually tweeted out a direct quote from the BlackRock recruiter, saying, "It's not who the president is—it's who's controlling the wallet of the president." And, "You got $10K? You can buy a senator."[5]

There was obviously some bravado in these claims, not to mention hyperbole, but there's no question that there was some truth in them as well. The one who controls the wallet can exert a whole lot of control.

As these things were coming to light, Fink claimed to have a change of heart. As Will Hild tweeted, "After we exposed the ESG scam for what it truly is, one of the main architects of the practice, @BlackRock CEO Larry Fink, said he's 'ashamed' to be a part of the debate. His scheme has been exposed and he knows it."[6]

As reported by Jerry Bowyer, "In an apparent culture war victory for conservatives, BlackRock CEO Larry Fink said he's throwing in the towel on ESG—environmental, social and governance—policies, in name at least, as a result of effective pushback against attempts by large asset managers such as BlackRock to force the adoption of woke standards that wouldn't otherwise be achievable through the democratic process."[7] (In a subsequent conversation, Fink claimed he never said he was ashamed and that he believed in "conscientious capitalism." But he added, "I'm not going to use the word ESG because it's been misused by the far left and the far right."[8])

Bowyer also explained that

> Blackrock is a Wall Street Behemoth, managing more of your pension dollars than any other company in the world. It led the way in pulling corporate America left, by pushing ESG—environmental, social and governance—investing.
>
> This approach takes the focus off of the fiduciary

responsibility to put the financial performance for your retirement funds above all else and shifts it towards various social goals. The backlash has been severe. (Bowyer also noted that "the left used [ESG] as a weapon. The right is just defending us against that.")[9]

Stop and think about that: BlackRock is managing a significant percentage of our pension dollars, which means that some major financial players will decide it's better to cooperate with BlackRock than to stand on principle, better to comply with their desires and keep the finances flowing. Why stir up such a powerful hornet's nest?

THE LOVE OF MONEY IS A ROOT
OF ALL KINDS OF EVIL

If you've followed my writings and radio commentary over the years, you know that I am not an economist. Far from it. That's why in the millions of words I have written in book and article form, along with the millions of words I have spoken, very few of them deal with the economy. But I do understand human nature. I do understand how much influence money can have, for good or for evil. And I do understand that money is a very effective cultural and political weapon. In fact, many elections come down to one question: Who has more money to spend on advertising?

That's why it's no surprise at all to hear these allegations about BlackRock forcing the behavior of big companies. Money talks, and quite loudly at that. Money actually shouts. If BlackRock feels that certain company policies are important, from promoting LGBTQ employees to investing funds to combat global warming, then they would expect the companies that get their money to promote those policies as well. Shall we call this financial bullying?

I wonder how many colleges and universities compromise their values to gain (or retain) major funding? "We don't want to offend our wealthy benefactors!" How many politicians tone down their messages to garner the big-dollar financial supporters? How many pastors and ministry leaders avoid controversial subjects, lest they alienate their wealthiest givers?[10] How many businesses take clear stands on current social issues *not* because they are morally convicted to do so but because it's financially expedient to do so? And what happens when, as noted in chapter 4, these stands begin to cost them dearly? Suddenly their tunes change. You can follow the money trail.

When I first got involved in pushing back against the gay activist agenda, I was surprised to see how popular it had become among the major companies, even in my home city, Charlotte, North Carolina. It almost seemed as if the companies were competing with one another to show how pro-gay they were. I addressed this in my 2007 lecture series "Homosexuality, the Church, and Society" (see chapter 3), devoting one entire night to the topic of corporate sponsorship of "diversity." I dove into this topic even more in my 2011 book *A Queer Thing Happened to America*.[11]

What quickly became apparent was the following: 1) Major companies, including giants such as Bank of America, IBM, and Blue Cross Blue Shield, believed this was the social and moral issue of the day, similar to the Civil Rights Movement of the 1960s. Gay *was* the new Black, and they were not going to be on the wrong side of history this time around. 2) Taking this position was very popular within the companies, since there were many talented LGBTQ workers in their midst.

Promoting them meant good business sense. 3) It was financially expedient to have a good track record when it came to gay (and then trans) rights. This was because already in 2007 the annual Corporate Equality Index, produced by the Human Rights Campaign (HRC), had become very influential. The higher you scored, the better your company's reputation. The lower you scored, the worse your reputation.

Two of my friends, themselves solid Christians and godly activists, attended the HRC's annual black-tie fundraising event in Charlotte in 2007 just to see things from the inside. They reported back to me in detail, telling me they had never witnessed such enthusiasm and unity, describing some of the videos shown during the dinner, including one from a leading bank. In these videos several LGBTQ+ employees were encouraged to "come out" together on the same day, thereby putting more pressure on the management to accept and affirm.

They also brought back samplings from many of the presentation tables at the event. These included material from Hotels.com, which gushed, "Thousands of gay-friendly hotel rooms and not a closet to be found among them. *Hotels.com is the ultimate source for gay-friendly hotels and is once again a proud sponsor of HRC.*" As for the *Charlotte Observer*, this well-known newspaper boasted that it had featured 187 articles on LGBT issues the previous year. Look at how LGBT-friendly we are!

In *A Queer Thing Happened to America*, I wrote:

> In 2002, the first year that the HRC issued its Corporate Equality Index, only *thirteen* major companies scored a perfect 100 (and remember that the HRC's guidelines were not as stringent back in 2002).

By 2010, the number had risen to *305*—an increase of better than 2300% in just eight years.

Just let your eyes scan this list of some of the best-known companies that scored 100% in 2010: 3M Co. * Abercrombie & Fitch * Aetna * Alaska Airlines * Alcoa * Allstate Corp. * American Express * American Airlines * Anheuser-Busch Companies * Apple * AT&T * Bank of America * Barnes & Noble * Bausch & Lomb * Best Buy * Boeing * Borders * Bristol-Myers Squibb Co. * Campbell Soup Co. * Capital One * Charles Schwab * Chevron * Chrysler * Cisco Systems * Citigroup * Clear Channel Communications * Clorox * Coca-Cola * Continental Airlines * Corning * Costco * Cox Enterprises * Dell * Deloitte & Touche * Delta Air Lines * Deutsche Bank * Dow Chemical * DuPont * Eastman Kodak * eBay Inc. * Ernst & Young * Estee Lauder * Esurance * Freddie Mac * Fannie Mae * Food Lion * Ford * Gap * General Mills * General Motors * Goldman Sachs * Google * Hallmark Cards * Harrah's * Hartford Financial Services * Health Care Service Corp. * Hewlett-Packard * Honeywell International * HSBC USA * Hyatt * ING North America Insurance * Intel * IBM * Intuit * J.P. Morgan Chase & Co. * JetBlue Airways * Johnson & Johnson * Kaiser Permanente * KeyCorp * Levi Strauss * LexisNexis * Liz Claiborne * Lockheed Martin Corp. * Macy * Marriott International * MasterCard * MetLife * Microsoft * MillerCoors * Monsanto * Morgan Stanley * Motorola * Nationwide * NCR * New York Life Insurance Co. * New York Times Co. * Newell Rubbermaid * Nielsen Co. * Nike * Nordstrom * Oracle * Orbitz * Owens Corning * Pacific Life Insurance * PepsiCo * Pfizer * PG&E * Pillsbury Winthrop Shaw Pittman * Procter & Gamble * Progressive Corp. * Prudential Financial

173

* Raytheon * Sears * Shell Oil * Sprint Nextel *
Starbucks * Starwood Hotels & Resorts Worldwide
* Subaru of America * Sun Life Financial Inc. * Sun
Microsystems * SunTrust Banks * Symantec Corp. *
Target * Texas Instruments * Time Warner * Toyota
Motor Sales USA * Travelport * United Parcel Service
* US Airways Group * Viacom * Visa * Volkswagen
of America * Walgreen * Walt Disney * Wells Fargo
& Co. * Whirlpool * Wynn Resorts * Xerox * Yahoo!
(Good luck trying to boycott all these companies!)[12]

The official HRC site explains:

> Launched in 2002, the HRC Foundation's Corporate
> Equality Index has become a roadmap and bench-
> marking tool for U.S. businesses in the evolving
> field of lesbian, gay, bisexual, transgender and queer
> equality in the workplace. The HRC Foundation is
> committed to keeping the criteria for the CEI rig-
> orous, fair and transparent by identifying emerging
> best practices that improve the experiences of
> LGBTQ employees of participating businesses.
> Equally important, we are committed to providing
> the resources and consultation that enable each busi-
> ness to attain a 100 percent rating.[13]

Yes, a perfect score is the goal.

As of 2023, "1,384 companies actively participated in
the CEI 2023–2024 Survey" (compare that with 305 in
2010!) Of those, "545 employers achieved a top score of
100 earning the coveted 'Equality 100 Award.'" In addition,
"378 Fortune 500 employers actively participated in the
2023–2024 CEI," and "163 American Law Magazine 200
law firms actively participated in the 2023–2024 CEI."[14]

Some aspects of the CEI are things all of us would affirm when it comes to treating all employees fairly. But for the most part the CEI grades businesses on very specific LGBTQ+ goals, such as *guaranteeing* that trans-identified people can use the bathroom of their choice (regardless of what hardship or trauma or discomfort it brings to other employees) or that these individuals *must* be called by their preferred name and gender pronoun, even if this changes several times in a year. If you want a perfect score, you had better comply. Once again, follow the money trail.

How Then Do We Respond?

I'm not writing as an economist since that is not my area of expertise. Instead, I'm writing based on biblical wisdom, common sense, and a burden from the Spirit.

First, Christian-owned companies must trust God for His blessing rather than bow to the pressure of investment firms such as BlackRock or activist groups such as the HRC. What we want is God's approval, not the world's, and if push comes to shove, we'd rather close down our businesses than compromise our values for the sake of the dollar. As followers of Jesus, there is no almighty dollar. There is only almighty God. If more and more companies, both faith based and secular, said, "Who cares about the Corporate Equality Index?" it would have less and less clout. (For the record, there was about a three-hundred-point drop from the 2022 Index to the new 2023–24 Index, as per the HRC update on November 30, 2023. Could this be a step in the right direction?)[15]

It's the same thing on the local, grassroots level. Small businesses must determine to do what is right, serving all customers as best as possible and not discriminating against anyone but refusing to compromise godly convictions (especially when it comes to participation in messages, expressions, or events that clearly contradict God's best for human flourishing), even under threat of potential loss of business or threat of a lawsuit. The example of the three Hebrew young men in Babylonian captivity should inspire us.

When faced with the threat of death if they refused to bow to a giant statue of the king—and it was a fiery death they were facing—they replied, "O Nebuchadnezzar, we have no need to answer you in this matter. If this be so, our God whom we serve is able to deliver us from the burning fiery furnace, and he will deliver us out of your hand, O king. But if not, be it known to you, O king, that we will not serve your gods or worship the golden image that you have set up" (Dan. 3:16–18, ESV). If enough of us respond in kind, the tide will quickly turn.

Second, Christian investment firms must keep their standards high, ensuring their investors that God's ways are best. I recently consulted for one such firm. (My assistant researched the company before I spoke with them. He told me they were serious players who had controlled several billion dollars. My services were provided gratis.) The representative who reached out to me said they were trying to determine where to draw the line in terms of recommendations for their Christian investors.

For example, let's say one company had developed an excellent nutritional product, but it was manufactured in China, using suspected child labor. Would that disqualify the company in their eyes? Or what if this company did not donate funds to LGBTQ+ causes, but every year during Pride Month they put up an affirming logo?

Should they be written off for this, despite the good products they sold? Or what if a company donated to both pro-life and pro-abortion organizations? What then?

While we talked through the specifics of numerous scenarios, one thing emerged clearly. Distinct lines needed to be drawn, even if this restricted their pool of potential investments for their clients. If they were going to be God honoring and Christian based, there was only one way to go. And without trying to force anyone's behavior, they could easily reach out to a company and say, "If you could remain neutral on some of these controversial topics, we would love to invest in your company since we like your products and services." We have our own money trail to follow.

Third, Christian-owned companies and businesses, along with individual Christian businesspeople, must recognize the divine calling on their lives, along with the sacred stewardship with which they have been entrusted. As I said in chapter 9 with reference to Christian educators, this too is a divine calling, a holy vocation. Or is all business worldly and of the devil while only the fivefold ministries are spiritual and holy?

Speaking candidly, I have not been the best fundraiser, even though our ministry is *very* frugal and the funds raised were not going in my own pocket. Still, when I asked for money, I did not make the strongest of appeals. What if the people themselves were hurting financially? How could I ask them for funds? As for the wealthy, I didn't want to pressure them to give.

While praying about all this in 2023, as I wrote this book, the Lord spoke to me strongly, especially about those with funds to spare: "It's not their money!" He said to me loudly and clearly. He had entrusted those funds to them, and when He wanted those funds for His work, He would let them know. It was their job to comply. My job was to proclaim the vision and share the need. He would speak to each one accordingly.

As for those who did give generously and even sacrificially (especially those with limited funds), He would bless them for it, either in this world or the world to come, or both. I already knew this, of course, but I had to renew my mind to these realities.

Remember that the company you run is not your company. It is the Lord's, and you are His steward. The business you own is not your business. It belongs to God. All the funds and assets you have, to the last penny, are the property of our heavenly Father. He has entrusted you with them, honoring your hard work, and even blessed you personally, but you are now the steward of those funds. Will you prove trustworthy?

Thankfully, there are thousands of godly businesspeople and countless companies owned by believers. Many are movers and shakers behind the scenes, donating tens of millions of dollars to world missions or humanitarian causes or good political candidates or righteous legal initiatives or Christian education or edifying movie productions or new business initiatives. They are being used by God and having a positive, transformative effect. We just need to see these efforts increase all the more.

Good things are happening, and the Jesus-based, ever-rising moral and cultural revolution is getting funded. But much more still needs to happen. May the funding take off dramatically in the coming years!

For more than a decade the primary funding for our ministry school came from one company in Ohio. The company had grown exponentially and supernaturally, and through the owner's generosity we were able to train, equip, and send out some of the finest Christian workers on the planet. What a great reward is in store for business-people who give like this.

There are godly voices that suddenly come to prominence on a national level. This is due of course to the blessing of God. But in some cases He used a wealthy Christian businessperson to back this godly leader, buying airtime for their ministry and helping to promote their message. Overnight their reach increased dramatically.

The same can happen on all the different fronts we'll outline in the final chapter of this book. So to each of you to whom God has entrusted funds and business influence, be prepared to be on the cutting edge of revolutionary cultural change. Your giving could be the key that unlocks the door. Let us forge the path of a new money trail! Your money, your talents, and your influence all belong to Him.

Back in 2019, *Forbes* reported,

> Over the next two decades, the United States will experience an unprecedented shift of demographics and finances that will likely be felt by every American.
>
> Baby Boomers, the generation of people born between 1944 and 1964, are expected to transfer $30 trillion in wealth to younger generations over the next many years. This jaw-dropping amount has led many journalists and financial experts to refer to the gradual event as the "great wealth transfer."
>
> In no prior time in the history of America has such a vast amount of wealth moved through the hands of generations.[16]

May that wealth transfer glorify the Lord, advance His kingdom, fuel the fires of a holy revolution, and make sense in the light of eternity. On with it!

CHAPTER 13

GETTING OUR MESSAGE
OUT TO THE NATION

JOHN WESLEY FAMOUSLY said:

> Do all the good you can,
> By all the means you can,
> In all the ways you can,
> In all the places you can,
> At all the times you can,
> To all the people you can,
> As long as ever you can.[1]

When it comes to getting our life-changing, society-impacting message out to the world, we must have the same mentality. Every one of us needs to use every means at our disposal everywhere we go, every day.

Working together, with each one in their proper lane, we can get this done. It just takes every single one of us doing our specific part, not under compulsion but out of love.

D. L. Moody is credited with saying, "I am only one, but I am one. I cannot do everything, but I can do something. What I can do, I ought to do, and what I ought to do, by the grace of God I will do."[2] If each one of us would do the "something" that we can, America would be transformed.

Together we must *infiltrate* all areas of society with our

message, *inundate* this lost world with life-giving truth, and *illuminate* this dying generation with a liberating word.

Infiltrate. Inundate. Illuminate. This is how we change the world, one heart and one mind at a time, always remembering *if we can change the way people think, we can change the way they live.*

What then would the Lord have you do? Where is your specific area of gifting? What is your circle of influence? How can you make a positive impact while you have breath, be it large or small? How can you help get the message out?

The light of one candle might not be that bright. But the light of tens of millions of candles cannot be ignored. It is high time we let our light shine—and that means your light and my light. Each of us must do our part.

Jesus taught that "the kingdom of heaven is like yeast that a woman took and mixed into about sixty pounds of flour until it worked all through the dough" (Matt. 13:33). How does the godly "yeast" of the gospel work its way through our society?

The yeast we have is supernaturally powerful and transformative, working just as effectively in every culture and in every age. How then do we "leaven" the masses? How do we fuel the fires of a lasting cultural awakening? How do we make our case to the nation? How do we blanket America with our message? People will not live differently unless they think differently, and so if we are to fulfill our calling as the salt of the earth and the light of the world, we must help people renew their minds.

Here are twelve essential gospel principles for getting our message out to the world:

1. We must keep our own batteries charged. As Jesus

said, "Be dressed ready for service and keep your lamps burning" (Luke 12:35). The simple truth is that we cannot give what we do not have, and we cannot bring others into something we are not experiencing. That's why it is so essential that we remain intimate with the Lord, not putting people under the yoke of religious tradition or imposing our moral standards on them. Instead, as people who radiate the life and love of Jesus, we attract people to His light.

No matter how grieved we might be by the deadly effects of sin, we must never forget that we are not called to be the morality police, patrolling our neighborhoods in search of anyone who violates our righteous rules. (In some Islamic countries, such as Iran and Saudi Arabia, the "morality police" really do exist, best known for enforcing strict dress codes on women.)[3] But if we do not walk in our first love for Jesus, which in turn produces a deep love for others, we can quickly degenerate into a bunch of self-righteous morality enforcers. This will only drive people away from our God rather than draw them to Him, repelling the very people we want to reach.

Paul wrote that "the fruit of the Spirit is love, joy, peace, forbearance, kindness, goodness, faithfulness, gentleness and self-control" (Gal. 5:22–23). This is the exact opposite of being mean-spirited, angry, judgmental, sour faced, and gloomy. In God's presence is fullness of joy (Ps. 16:11), and the joy of the Lord is our strength (Neh. 8:10). Paul actually *commanded* us to be joyful, writing, "Rejoice in the Lord always. I will say it again: Rejoice! Let your gentleness be evident to all. The Lord is near" (Phil. 4:4–5; remember that he wrote these words from a prison in Rome). And despite the many hardships he endured and the heavy burdens he carried, he described himself as "sorrowful, yet always rejoicing" (2 Cor. 6:10). What an example for each of us!

But we can do this only by focusing on the Lord, spending quality time with Him, and renewing our own hearts and minds. Rejoice! He is good! He is beautiful! He gives life! He forgives! He transforms! That's our Savior! That's our God! And we are His representatives here on earth, introducing Him to others and "selling" His "product," so to speak.

Are we offering stale bread to the world or the Bread of Life? Are we preaching a system of rules and regulations or bringing people into a life-transforming divine encounter? Do people who listen to our message and watch our lives conclude that God is love? Or do they conclude that He is a grouchy, never-satisfied deity who hates everyone and delights in their demise?

For sure, our message calls out sin and confronts unrighteousness. We do not dilute the truth or lower the standards of God. But if we are walking in love, joy, peace, forbearance, kindness, goodness, faithfulness, gentleness, and self-control—if we ourselves are full of the Spirit, radiating the kindness and compassion of the Lord—many will listen and many will be changed. Our message will bring life to the degree that we ourselves are alive.

The bottom line is that as salt, we must keep our saltiness, and as light, we must shine brightly. That means we must keep our batteries charged.

2. We must believe in our own message. Sometimes we forget how wonderful the gospel is. Sometimes we forget that God's ways are best and that in Jesus we have the words of eternal life. Sometimes we forget that our message brings hope and redemption, reconciliation and transformation, and that the Bible is the preeminent book of wisdom on the planet.

One great way to remind ourselves of the beauty of the Lord and the power of the gospel is by sharing testimonies. The more we hear about what God is doing, the more encouraged we become—and the more stoked we get about the good news. How amazing it is to see the tears of gratitude, to hear the shouts of joy, to witness people of all ages getting free from their addictions, their bondages, their fears, their sins—all as a direct result of them responding to the message we preach and teach and live.

Young people today in America are more stressed, depressed, anxious, lonely, and suicidal than any generation in recorded history. Jesus really is the answer to their problems and pain, as opposed to simply being the head of a worldwide religion. Let us renew our excitement about the message we bring!

3. We must evangelize everywhere. On the most fundamental level, this is how we change the nation, as rebels are made righteous and sinners become saints (to use New Testament language; see 1 Corinthians 1:2–3, NKJV). This is something we can all do.

Do you have a testimony of how the Lord has changed your own life? You can share your story with someone else. It is the most fundamental way we bear witness, telling others what we have seen and experienced in our own lives.

Many times when someone I've just met offers me a cup of coffee, I reply, "Actually, I've never had a cup of coffee in my life." This normally shocks them. I then say, "I've never smoked a cigarette either." Now they're even more surprised. Then I say, "But I was shooting heroin at the age of fifteen," which leads naturally into my own testimony.

Maybe your testimony is not as dramatic as mine, but if Jesus has changed your own life, if He has healed your body, if He has worked a miracle on your behalf, if He has been with you in the darkest of times, you have a story to tell as well. Look for opportunities to make Him known. We are called to be fishers of men and women (Luke 5:10).

Do we have a nonbelieving friend or neighbor or coworker or family member or teammate or fellow student? Do we meet new people from time to time? We should be praying for opportunities and looking for opportunities to share the good news with them.

We can even start Bible studies in our schools, in our gyms, in our places of business, in our homes, or online— really, we can do this anywhere. Or we can invite people to the meetings we attend. In fact, one of the most effective ways to make an impact on college campuses is through evangelistic study groups, since it may take us decades to bring a healthy balance to the school's faculty. But we can get our message out *today* by doing campus outreach. This is just one potential example among many.

The reality is that the most fruitful evangelism is relational, normally done in the context of work or family life. We hang out with our friends and family members and coworkers. We build relationships with one another. We live life, on some level, together. This is the greatest field of all for evangelism. Let us share the gospel everywhere. It is literally the difference between eternal life and eternal death.

What if we had the cure for cancer and everyone in our neighborhood or workplace or school was dying of that foul disease? Would we keep the cure to ourselves out of fear that people would not believe us or might reject us?

Wouldn't our love for them override all such concerns? The message of the life, death, and resurrection of Jesus is infinitely greater than a cure for cancer. Let us share it everywhere we go, as the Lord gives grace and as the circumstances allow.

As Salvation Army cofounder William Booth (1829–1912) urged his workers with great passion "Go straight for souls, and go for the worst."[4] Or, as C. H. Spurgeon, known as the Prince of Preachers, reminded us, "I would sooner bring one sinner to Jesus Christ than unravel all the mysteries of the divine Word, for salvation is the one thing we are to live for."[5]

4. We must make our case to the nation. Two thousand years ago Peter urged his readers to "revere Christ as Lord" and "always be prepared to give an answer to everyone who asks you to give the reason for the hope that you have. But do this with gentleness and respect, keeping a clear conscience, so that those who speak maliciously against your good behavior in Christ may be ashamed of their slander" (1 Pet. 3:15–16).

The Greek word for *answer* is *apologia*, from which we get the word *apologetics*. But this is not an apology for our faith. Quite the contrary. It is the rational defense of our faith. It is our robust answer to the critics and skeptics and seekers and mockers as we declare with both confidence and humility, "We are on the side of truth! Allow us to explain."

The word *apologia* is used in Acts 22:1, where Paul said to the large Jewish crowd in Jerusalem, "Listen now to my *defense*" (emphasis added). It is the word used in 1 Corinthians 9:3, where Paul wrote, "This is my *defense* to those who sit in judgment on me" (emphasis added). It is the word he uses in 2 Timothy 4:16, speaking of his trial in Rome: "At my first *defense*, no one came to my support" (emphasis added). And it is the word Paul used when writing to the Philippians from his prison cell in Rome, saying, "It is right for me to feel this way about all of you, since I have you in my heart and, whether I am in chains or *defending* and confirming the gospel, all of you share in God's grace with me" (Phil. 1:7, emphasis added). He also stated that he was in prison "for the *defense* of the gospel" (Phil. 1:16, emphasis added). I think you get the feel for the meaning of the word!

We are on trial before the world. We are told that the Bible is unreliable and irrelevant, that the God of the Bible is hateful and petty, that our faith is based on myths and fables, that there are many pagan parallels to Jesus, that science disproves the Scriptures, that all world religions are alike, that our message doesn't really work, that the church hurts people rather than helps people. The list goes on and on.

But we have an answer. We have a defense. For every attack, we have a counterattack—and a winning one at that. We have an *apologia*!

One of the most effective things we can do in making our case to the nation is point to the trajectory of a belief or mindset or lifestyle. Multiply this over and over, and where does it lead? The trajectory of our faith, multiplied endlessly, brings endlessly good results and leads to human flourishing. The trajectory of anti-God, anti-faith philosophies and ideologies and practices leads to confusion, dissolution, the breakdown of families, the decay of institutions, and the destruction of a nation. We are not only on the side of truth; we are on the side of life.

Let us then make our case to the nation on every platform available, advocating for the sanctity of life (beginning in the womb), advocating for God's plan for marriage and sexuality, advocating for the truth of His Word. We need not cower in fear. We need not feel ashamed and ill-equipped. The truth sets people free (John 8:31–32), and in the end nothing can be done against the truth (2 Cor. 13:8). America can be changed if we simply tell the truth.

If some of us feel we are not well equipped to answer the critics and respond to the challenging questions—after all, not all of us are called to be apologists—we simply need to 1) be aware that answers *do* exist, and 2) point people to web pages such as askdrbrown.org/recommendedresources where scores of excellent resources are listed dealing with the major objections to our faith.

Not that long ago, the writings of the so-called "new atheists" were captivating millions, but while these God-mocking critics were experts in tearing down, they were novices at building back up. What hope and life and joy and goodness and transforming power did they leave in their wake? None that meet the deepest needs of our lives or will stand the test of time.[6] We have a better way—one that is sound intellectually and spiritually, morally and experientially. Let us continue to present our case to the nation.

5. We must regain our prophetic voice. In his thunderous 1970 book *How Black Is the Gospel*, evangelist Tom Skinner wrote,

> Many black Americans bitterly denounce Christianity and the Bible because, in their view, those who practice religious piety are among the leading exponents of hate, bigotry and prejudice. They feel that these "Bible-toting Saints" perpetuate

the most segregated hour of the week—eleven o'clock Sunday morning.

Today's young blacks, having learned more history than their forebears, are quick to resent acts of so called Christianity and the use of those random Biblical verses that are so blatantly detrimental to the dignity of the black man in America.

There must have been thousands of slaves who vowed when they learned to read that they would never look at or allow their children to see those passages of St. Paul, which encourage servants to be obedient to their masters. In many instances, these were the only portions of the Bible that "ole massa" would allow the preacher to read to illiterate black men, in the hope that obedience to the Scriptures would further secure the system of white supremacy. This spirit still lives.[7]

He adds,

Many whites were convinced that black people, commonly referred to as "they," would never have become concerned about their civil rights in the first place had not the Communists stirred them up. Black clergymen who become involved in the cause were considered by many whites to be agitators who left their calling to meddle in matters clearly outside the will of God. "What those people need is the gospel."[8]

He writes as if the gospel did not intersect with issues such as slavery and segregation.

These are cutting, caustic words, a strong rebuke from a Jesus-preaching, Bible-believing man of God. But Skinner did not stop there.

> One thing is certain: whatever contemporary man decides about the "color" of religion, Christ stands outside that debate. Even a superficial reading of the gospel reveals that Christ showed only one, special interest—allegiance to His Father and the Kingdom of God. He was owned by no man, He belonged to no particular group, and He refused to sanction one party or system over another. He was God in the form of man—neither black nor white....
>
> Christ taught His followers to be just in their dealings with and to love each other. Leadership was redefined in terms of service, and labor was elevated from an exercise in self-interest to a means of helping those in need. Family relations were hallowed and sex given a Godly status. This transforms the issue of politics and economics from a reluctant response to law to a wholesome affirmation of love for one's fellow man. Brotherly love, as it is commonly known, is extended to embrace all men.[9]

We need more voices like Skinner's today, voices that confront both the church and the world, not with partisan politics or human grudges but with piercing, prophetic truth. We also need more contemporary voices such as theologian and philosopher Francis Schaeffer, who saw where society was heading and warned us in advance.

Let us then cut through the social madness with eye-opening revelation. Let us dispel the darkness with liberating light. Let us expose the lies with holy, inconvenient truth. Let us rebuke worldly injustice while we model biblically based justice. Let us uncover what is wrong and reveal what is right. If we do not do this—we who have the Word of God and the Spirit of God—then who will? And if we don't do this today, when America remains deeply fractured along racial, ethnic, moral, cultural, and spiritual lines, then when?

Many times Christians are perceived as keepers of the status quo. In reality, the gospel message is revolutionary, the ultimate threat to all man-made kingdoms and systems. May we recover the prophetic nature of the gospel, which makes both sinners and saints uncomfortable. May we declare what is coming before it happens, thereby getting the world's attention in order to ask, "Will you listen to us now?" May we, above all people in America, be truly revolutionary, not through rebellion and resentment, and not with carnal weapons such as violence and intimidation—God forbid!—but with radical obedience to the commands of Jesus. On with the revolution!

6. We must disciple millions through movies and songs. We all know the power of movies and songs. They move us and influence us deeply, whether we are fully conscious of their impact or not. That's why I wrote a book titled *The Power of Music: God's Call to Change the World One Song at a Time*. As much as I wrote the book out of my own personal experience and based on the knowledge I had, doing further research was incredibly eye-opening. Music is even more powerful than I realized! And I could have just as easily written a book called *The Power of Movies: God's Call to Change the World One Film at a Time* had this been an area of focus for me over the years.

The movies we watch and the songs we listen to are reflections of the culture in which we live. But these movies and songs also help *shape* culture.

When it comes to movies, an article on the Platt College website notes, "*Fight Club* inspired fight clubs in real life....*The Thin Blue Line* shook our faith in police....*The Day After Tomorrow* brought global warming to life....*V for Vendetta* inspire[d] hacktivist group Anonymous.... *Bambi* causes a drop in hunting....*Jaws* takes a bite out of beach vacations....*Blackfish* makes us see Sea World differently."

Yes, "Films of any genre, from documentary to drama, can have a dramatic impact on real life. Chances are excellent that you've seen at least one film that has changed the landscape of our popular culture, even if you're not aware of it. These films that have changed our lives outside the theater in tangible ways are excellent examples of the important role film plays in the world at large."[10]

As for music, where do I start? I can point to two major songs that were credited with ending the war in Vietnam in the 1960s.[11] I can point to a chart-topping song on being born gay or trans that greatly influenced the thinking of young people.[12] I can point to hip-hop songs that degrade women in coarse and obscene ways or call for violence against police[13]—just to mention a few examples of many.

On the gospel side of things, when it comes to movies I can point to the influence of contemporary films such as *The Jesus Revolution* and *Sound of Freedom*, which have impacted both believers and nonbelievers. When it comes to music I can point to the endless stream of powerful worship songs, written to be sung by believers, along with crossover music like that of the Christian rock band

Skillet, reaching a wider audience and speaking in more generic terms about our sin-sick condition and need for a Savior. (John Cooper, the frontman of Skillet, uses his large platform to preach Jesus clearly and to combat woke ideologies in the church.)[14]

Thankfully, there is an increase today in films with an overt Christian message, including movies such as *The Case for Christ*, which recounts the personal testimony of Lee Strobel, and the *God's Not Dead* series, which has also served as a platform for effective campus outreach.[15] And there are Christian-based movies that address key social issues (such as the pro-life film *Unplanned*), along with those that don't directly preach the gospel but point to a Christian worldview or carry a strong moral and inspirational message (such as the recent movie *Sound of Freedom*).[16]

7. We must flood social media with our stories. Hundreds of millions of Jesus followers use social media worldwide. It's important that we pray about the best way to use these platforms, since billions of people are heavily influenced by them. Just think of the destructive effects of some of the TikTok videos I cited in chapter 7.

The key thing today is to tell our stories, since those stories, more than almost any number of statistics, will impact society and change people's perceptions and beliefs. It is personal stories that changed people's perceptions about homosexuality, ranging from "My relationship with my partner is no different than your (heterosexual) relationship with your partner" to "I'm born this way and cannot change." Put another way, gay is good, and being gay is innate and immutable.

Or, in the case of transgender identity, "I realized I was

trapped in the wrong body and lived in torment for years. When I finally discovered the truth and transitioned, it set me free." Who can argue with someone's personal story?[17]

The fact is that we have endless stories of our own: stories of being set free from every addiction and sin, stories of being transformed from depression to joy and from suicide to a passion for life, stories of having our doubts resolved with the discovery of truth, stories of coming out of homosexuality, stories of the false promises of transitioning and the power of being healed from the inside out. Let us continue to flood the internet with our personal, God-glorifying, hope-imparting stories!

The more we get our stories out on social media and other online platforms—as well as through traditional print, video, and audio formats—the more we will change the way people think, thereby changing the way they live.

8. We must form authentic communities that become the core of our movement. As I stated earlier, our emphasis must be on *being* the church rather than on *going to* church, since we are, above all, a community and a family. Regardless of age, ethnicity, or gender, the vast majority of people are drawn to community—to loving, caring, lasting, authentic relationships. We want to feel loved and valued. We want to care for others. We want to be part of something bigger than ourselves. We want to have a purpose. We want our lives to count. We want to have a place.

This is why so many young people threw themselves into BLM and Antifa. It gave them a sense of purpose and connected them with others who wanted to make a difference. It gave them a cause to fight for, even if they went about things in wrong and destructive ways, and even though many of their goals were deeply misguided.[18]

When it comes to the gospel, these same young people will be drawn to authentic community, especially if it has purpose and meaning, and especially if the people in that community want to make an impact on the society. But isn't this exactly what the body of Christ should be—the ultimate family that truly loves and cares, the ultimate community that makes a difference in the world?

Danish theologian Søren Kierkegaard wrote, "The thought of Christianity was to want to change everything....Twelve men united on being Christians have recreated the face of the world."[19] Commenting on this, Os Guinness noted, "Indeed, that transforming power is at the heart of the genius of the West, and a direct gift of the gospel with its emphasis on life change. In Christopher Dawson's words, 'Western civilization has been the great ferment of change in the world, because the changing of the world became an integral part of its cultural ideal.'"[20] Well said!

This call to change the world is in our blood, not by domination or intimidation but by example and message and service and the Spirit. That's why when we see injustice, we want to confront it. When we see that something is not right, we want to fix it. When we encounter poverty and pain, we want to alleviate it. When we see people lost and confused, we want to help them find their way. We are like doctors and nurses on a medical missions trip. We have the tools. We have the medicine. We have the antidote. We are here to help people get healthy!

We feel this way because we are created in the image of God, because Jesus lives inside us, because the Spirit does

His work through us. In a very real way we are the Lord's hands and feet, doing His will on the earth in the here and now. How then can we make Him known to the world? How can we demonstrate His love? How can we emulate His actions? How can we display His character? How can we be lights in dark places? How can we liberate the captives? How can we carry out His plan of redemption?

To quote Os Guinness again: "If Christians are living as 'salt and light' in any society, and they reach a critical mass where they are more than a small counterculture, then the 'Christianness' or otherwise of that society (the degree to which that society reflects the way of Jesus) is a test of the degree to which Christians are living out the way of Jesus in obedience."[21]

And how exactly do we do this? Here's the biblical battle plan. You've heard it before, but this time think in terms of God's method for bringing about revolutionary change:

> So Christ himself gave the apostles, the prophets, the evangelists, the pastors and teachers, to equip his people for works of service, so that the body of Christ may be built up until we all reach unity in the faith and in the knowledge of the Son of God and become mature, attaining to the whole measure of the fullness of Christ.
>
> Then we will no longer be infants, tossed back and forth by the waves, and blown here and there by every wind of teaching and by the cunning and craftiness of people in their deceitful scheming. Instead, speaking the truth in love, we will grow to become in every respect the mature body of him who is the head, that is, Christ. From him the whole body, joined and

held together by every supporting ligament, grows and builds itself up in love, *as each part does its work.*

—EPHESIANS 4:11–16, EMPHASIS ADDED

Let each of us, then, do our part. If we do, our nation will look very different tomorrow than it does today. In this regard, I have often quoted the words of Yale law professor Stephen L. Carter, who said,

> Radical transformation will demand a sacrifice. But a fundamental demand for sacrifice will not arise in politics. It will have to arise from the church, which is really the only contemporary, genuine source of resistance to the existing order. Nobody else can do it. Nobody was ever persuaded to go out and risk life and limb because of reading a smart article on philosophy and public affairs. No people ever said they were going to organize a march and be beaten by the police because of something they read in *The New York Times* op-ed page. It is only religion that still has the power, at its best, to encourage sacrifice and resistance.[22]

The church must lead the way.

9. We must invest billions of dollars into godly messaging. In the previous chapter we emphasized the power of money in changing society as companies and individuals invest their funds in specific causes to advance their particular agendas. Here I will simply say this to every Christian businessperson and company and firm: Please don't let the nonbelieving, often greedy, sometimes power-hungry people of this world use their money and talents with a greater sense of purpose than you do as kingdom-minded, eternity-grounded children of God. Let your money count!

As someone who carries a message that burns in my heart day and night, I appeal to each of you. We need your help and support! We cannot do this on our own. We may have the words, but you can help us magnify those words. We may have the voice, but you can help us amplify that voice. We may have a dream, but you can help bring that dream to reality. We may have a burden and a cause, but we need your expertise, your vision, and your funding to see the mission through. I urge you, as stewards of God's resources and giftings, to make your decisions in the light of eternity. We really do need your help!

This is holy teamwork, a sacred partnership. Together we can make a difference, both in this world and in the world to come. Let us get on with it!

10. We must reeducate the nation. In chapters 7–9 we focused on the assault on our children and what we can do in response, including making a greater impact on the educational systems of America as parents, teachers, administrators, counselors, librarians, and more—from preschool to grad school and from home school to public school. And by God's grace this is exactly what we will continue to do.

But why stop there? Someone has to provide textbooks for classes—not just for Christian schools and homeschool networks (which we have been doing for years) but for secular schools as well. Why can't we write those books? Why can't we create new curricula? Why can't we help reeducate the nation?

One of my colleagues is a leader in his state's public education system, helping to craft balanced curricula for all the schools. Although the classes themselves are secular in nature and he cannot insert his own faith perspective, he *can* ensure that the courses are balanced and truthful, and he *can* provide a sober, educated counter voice to the radical voices that so dominate the educational system. In that respect he is like a Joseph or Daniel, serving in an influential position in a "pagan" culture and system, so there are many challenges along the way. But what a great position to hold!

I'm sure my friend is just one among many believers in similar situations. I encourage you to embrace your calling as the Lord's representative, not viewing your job as simply a way to make a living but also a way to change hearts and minds. May the Lord use you mightily!

Another colleague has coauthored Black History 365 (BH365), "a U.S. History textbook and ebook/app documenting the unique stories of Black persons, groups, and cultures in North America, beginning in Ancient Africa continuing to modern events and movements....The gateway to connecting history to daily life, this transcendent approach to American history allows students of all ethnicities to engage in meaningful conversations with teachers, peers, and their families...through the lens of Black History."[23]

As of July 2023, the BH365 K–12 Curriculum and Resource was being used in more than two hundred school districts across the country. May it increase and multiply, along with other resources that will help reeducate the nation based on rational truth rather than radical ideology.

11. We must all speak up. After the British Christian politician King Lawal "was reportedly canceled by seven different organizations and suspended by his own political party for tweeting out his religious views," he said,

"First of all, I am still feeling quite upset. But I'm so ready to fight back, as well. I'm not wanting to be silenced anymore, and I'm wanting to see more Christians stand up and fight back."[24] Yes! This is so essential if we are to get our message out, refusing to be intimidated by cancel culture, refusing to be silenced. More Christians must stand up, speak up, and fight back.

Lawal rightly stated that "there is an intensified erosion of our rights to speak freely; freedom of speech, freedom of expression and belief. And it's going out of control a bit." This is actually quite an understatement today. Things are more than "out of control a bit" when it comes to the attacks on our freedoms.

But our freedoms can only be canceled with our cooperation and consent. That's because you can cancel or silence one or two, but you cannot cancel or silence tens of millions.

All of us have to speak up, from kids in schools to moms and dads in their neighborhoods (and homes), from professors on campus to doctors and nurses in the hospitals, from newscasters to sportscasters, athletes to social media influencers, cooks to cleaners, and pilots to painters. Whoever we are, wherever we are, with one voice we must say we are not backing down or bowing down, cowering or capitulating.

Really now, what would happen if everyone were honest enough to say, "The emperor has no clothes! Those new clothes are not clothes at all!" The sham would end right there.

It was to encourage Christian boldness that we launched the annual Not Ashamed of Jesus Day every April 14, based on Esther 4:14, where Mordecai reminds Queen Esther that she was brought into the kingdom for such a time as this. I also devoted a chapter to this in my book *The Silencing of the Lambs: The Ominous Rise of Cancel Culture and How We Can Overcome It*. As we explain on our website:

> On that day, every single one of us, in whatever way we can, will let the world know that Jesus is our Lord and our Master and our Savior and our Deliverer and our King, and we are not ashamed to be identified with Him. Let the whole world know that we are His!
>
> You might say, "But shouldn't we do that every day? Shouldn't we look for opportunities to lift up the Lord every day of the week? Shouldn't we always be known as believers?"
>
> Absolutely, we should, as the Lord leads and as the doors are open. Being witnesses is our 24/7 calling 365 days a year.
>
> But here's the thing. Many of us have floated under the radar for years. Our colleagues at work don't know we are believers. Our friends don't know about our faith, at least, the depth of our faith. Our neighbors are unaware that we are believers. We may be sincere, but we are stealth....
>
> So let's make a statement on April 14, and let's live by that statement every day of the year. And let's refuse to be silenced or cancelled.[25]

May all of us, at the right time and in the right spirit, raise our voices as one. To say it again, together we cannot be canceled or silenced.

12. We must lose our lives for the gospel. The second half of my book *The Silencing of the Lambs* lists many practical strategies for overcoming cancel culture. But they all come down to this principle: we must take up our crosses and deny ourselves if we are to be genuine followers of Jesus. We must lose our lives for the gospel if we want to really find our lives. It is the only way. That's why one university professor was right in calling for Kamikaze Academics, urging his fellow professors to speak up, no matter the cost. (His own challenges to global warming theories—as a scientist himself—cost him dearly.)[26]

Yale law professor Stephen Carter, who calls for churches to be "centers of resistance," also warns that "one should have no illusions. All too many pastors today, black and white, are so worried about filling the seats. Clergy deliver brilliant sermons that preach up to the edge of asking people to do something, and then they will pull back. Some pastors display prophetic leadership and call for sacrifice, but their numbers are small."[27]

May we have more of these courageous pastors today. May we have more believers who determine that Jesus is worth living for and dying for. May we recognize that the purpose of our lives is to glorify God, whatever the cost or consequence.

Can we justify our silence out of fear that we might lose our friends on social media when our brothers and sisters around the world are losing their lives for Him? Can we justify our cowardice (often in the guise of "wisdom") while standing at the foot of the cross and looking into the light of eternity? In the words of the Methodist preacher W. E. Sangster (1900–1960), "How shall I feel at the judgment, if multitudes of missed opportunities pass before me in full review, and all my excuses prove to be disguises of my cowardice and pride?"[28]

For good reason, a Catholic leader wrote in July 2023, "If we don't stand for what we believe, then our society will be swept away, taking all of us along with it."[29] And after a young man was arrested for reading the Bible outside a public drag queen event, where obscene acts took place in the presence of little children, he said, "It was worth it. It's actually an honor to be counted worthy to stand with the cloud of witnesses who have gone before us and been arrested for the sake of spreading Christ and his kingdom. If the police wanted to try and set an example for others or anything like that, the only thing I've seen is actually the exact opposite, where more and more people are seeing the severity of what's going on and being called to more action."[30]

This too is how we get our message out: nothing can intimidate us, and we are not going in the closet. We have already committed our hearts and minds and souls to the Lord, and we are determined to stand.

It was these words, spoken in a 2016 TV interview, that helped propel University of Toronto professor Jordan Peterson to international stardom. He was asked what he was willing to suffer in defiance of a new law in Canada that would require him to use certain terminology if a trans-identified person insisted on it. He said, "If they fine me, I won't pay it. If they put me in jail, I'll go on a hunger strike. I'm not doing this. And that's that. I'm not using the words that other people require me to use. Especially if they're made up by radical left-wing ideologues."[31] And Peterson said this without even being a Christian at that point in his life. This was simply his moral conviction.

We can be loving toward all and compassionate and sensitive. But if we're asked to violate our conscience or our convictions, we say with all respect, "I'm sorry, but I cannot comply. I have a higher allegiance." May we all live lives worthy of the Lord!

Following Jesus has always been a revolutionary act, not in the sense of rebellion but in the sense of radicality, and the real gospel message has always had a revolutionary effect on the society. Will we live it out today? If not us, then who? If not now, then when?

These questions are all the more urgent during seasons of spiritual outpouring, which is why my last book (and the first in this series on moving from revival to reformation) is titled *Seize the Moment: How to Fuel the Fires of Revival*. Now, as the Spirit is moving afresh in the land, we must seize the holy moment of revival and build on the holy momentum of revival. We must turn the tide!

The pushback has begun, and the long-awaited, gospel-based moral and cultural revolution has begun. It is time for us to lead the way! Can I count you in? More importantly, can our God count you in? You have come into the kingdom for such a time as this!

NOTES

Preface

1. Leonard Ravenhill, "The Opportunity of a Lifetime...," QuoteFancy, accessed February 1, 2024, https://quotefancy.com/quote/2470927/Leonard-Ravenhill-The-opportunity-of-a-lifetime-needs-to-be-seized-during-the-lifetime-of.

Chapter 1

1. Michael L. Brown, PhD, *Revival or We Die: A Great Awakening Is Our Only Hope* (Shippensburg, PA: Destiny Image, 2021).
2. Amanda L. Giordano, PhD, LPC, "What to Know About Adolescent Pornography Exposure," *Psychology Today*, February 27, 2022, https://www.psychologytoday.com/us/blog/understanding-addiction/202202/what-know-about-adolescent-pornography-exposure.
3. "What's the Average Age of a Child's First Exposure to Porn?," Fight the New Drug, accessed November 10, 2023, https://fightthenewdrug.org/real-average-age-of-first-exposure.
4. "Unmarried Childbearing," National Center for Health Statistics, accessed November 10, 2023, https://www.cdc.gov/nchs/fastats/unmarried-childbearing.htm.
5. Michelle Castillo, "Almost Half of First Babies in U.S. Born to Unwed Mothers," CBS News, March 15, 2013, https://www.cbsnews.com/news/almost-half-of-first-babies-in-us-born-to-unwed-mothers; Cheryl Wetzstein, "Census: More First-Time Mothers Give Birth Out of Wedlock," *Washington Times*, July 8, 2014, http://www.washingtontimes.com/news/2014/jul/8/census-more-first-time-mothers-give-birth-out-of-wedl/?page=all. For disturbing stats from the UK, see Joe Davies, "Majority of Babies Were Born Out of Wedlock in 2021 for the First Time on Record," *Daily Mail*, August 9, 2022, https://www.dailymail.co.uk/health/article-11095693/More-babies-born-wedlock-2021-time-record.html. More broadly, see Joe Carter, "9 Things You Should Know About Out-of-Wedlock Births," TGC,

November 3, 2018, https://www.thegospelcoalition.org/article/9-things-you-should-know-about-out-of-wedlock-births.

6. Castillo, "Almost Half of First Babies in U.S. Born to Unwed Mothers."

7. Stephanie Kramer, "U.S. Has World's Highest Rate of Children Living in Single-Parent Households," Pew Research Center, December 12, 2019, https://www.pewresearch.org/short-reads/2019/12/12/u-s-children-more-likely-than-children-in-other-countries-to-live-with-just-one-parent.

8. Frank Newport, "Slowdown in the Rise of Religious Nones," Gallup, December 9, 2022, https://news.gallup.com/opinion/polling-matters/406544/slowdown-rise-religious-nones.aspx.

9. Gregory A. Smith, "About Three-in-Ten U.S. Adults Are Now Religiously Unaffiliated," Pew Research Center, December 14, 2021, https://www.pewresearch.org/religion/2021/12/14/about-three-in-ten-u-s-adults-are-now-religiously-unaffiliated.

10. John Woodrow Cox et al., "More Than 357,000 Students Have Experienced Gun Violence at School Since Columbine," *Washington Post*, updated October 6, 2023, https://www.washingtonpost.com/education/interactive/school-shootings-database.

11. Catherine Stoddard, "List: The Most Deadly US Mass School Shootings," Fox 7 Austin, May 24, 2022, https://www.fox7austin.com/news/list-the-most-deadly-us-mass-school-shootings.

12. David Marcus, "Anarchy in the USA," *Daily Mail*, June 4, 2023, https://www.dailymail.co.uk/news/article-12157707/DAVID-MARCUS-Anarchy-USA-100-billion-year-stolen-dystopian-stores-lock-goods.html.

13. Tim Drake, "Cardinal George: The Myth and Reality of 'I'll Die in My Bed,'" *National Catholic Register*, April 17, 2015, https://www.ncregister.com/blog/cardinal-george-the-myth-and-reality-of-ill-die-in-my-bed.

14. Michael L. Brown, PhD, *Saving a Sick America: A Prescription for Moral and Cultural Transformation* (Nashville, TN: Nelson Books, 2017), 178–189.

15. Greg Myre, "How the Soviet Union's Collapse Explains the Current Russia-Ukraine Tension," NPR, December 24, 2021, https://www.npr.org/2021/12/24/1066861022/how-the-soviet-unions-collapse-explains-the-current-russia-ukraine-tension.

16. Joe Carter, "20 Key Quotes From Alexander Solzhenitsyn's Harvard Address," Religion & Liberty Online, June 8, 2018, https://rlo.acton.org/archives/101976-20-key-quotes-from-alexander-solzhenitsyns-harvard-address.html.

17. Elliot Clark, "Francis Schaeffer Warned Us About 2020," TGC, December 9, 2020, https://www.thegospelcoalition.org/reviews/church-end-20th-century-francis-shaeffer.

18. Jacob Geanous, "Woman Pressured Into Breast Removal at 13 Under 'Erroneous Belief' She Was Transgender: Lawsuit," *NY Post*, June 18, 2023, https://nypost.com/2023/06/17/woman-sues-hospital-for-removing-her-breasts-when-she-was-13-years-old.

19. Michael Brown, "Radical Transgender Activism Is Proof Positive That We Have Lost Our Corporate Minds," *Christian Post*, July 15, 2021, https://www.christianpost.com/voices/transgender-activism-is-proof-that-we-have-lost-our-minds.html.

20. Mikael Wood, "'WAP' Makes It Rain, Breaks Streaming Record en Route to No. 1 on Billboard Hot 100," *Los Angeles Times*, August 17, 2020, https://www.latimes.com/entertainment-arts/music/story/2020-08-17/wap-cardi-b-megan-thee-stallion-number-one-billboard-hot-100.

21. Audrey Conklin, "Fentanyl Overdoses Become No. 1 Cause of Death Among US Adults, Ages 18–45: 'A National Emergency,'" Fox News, December 16, 2021, https://www.foxnews.com/us/fentanyl-overdoses-leading-cause-death-adults.

22. Michael Brown, "An Inauguration to Make Orwell Proud," Townhall, January 14, 2013, https://townhall.com/columnists/michaelbrown/2013/01/14/an-inauguration-to-make-orwell-proud-n1488760.

23. Michael L. Brown, "Why Celebrating the Sisters of Perpetual Indulgence Was a Step Too Far," Charisma News, June 2, 2023, https://www.charismanews.com/opinion/in-the-line-of-fire/92430-why-celebrating-the-sisters-of-perpetual-indulgence-was-a-step-too-far.

24. "Witchcraft Rises Among Millennials, Thanks to Hollywood Movies," Everyday Christian Parent, May 24, 2022, https://www.everydaychristianparent.com/witch-atheists-presbyterians-hollywood-wicca-movies.

25. Email titled "Bring on the Counterrevolution," August 9, 2023. The abbreviations cited stand for Critical Race Theory (CRT); Diversity, Equity, Inclusion (DEI); Environmental, Social, and Governance (ESG). For more, see Christopher F. Rufo, *America's Cultural Revolution* (New York: HarperCollins, 2023).

CHAPTER 2

1. Michael L. Brown, *The Revival Answer Book: Rightly Discerning the Contemporary Revival Movements* (Ventura, CA: Renew Books,

2001), 14–15. I cited from J. Wesley Bready, *This Freedom Whence* (Winona Lake, IN: Light and Life Press, 1950), 93–97.

2. Michael L. Brown, *The Revival Answer Book* (Ada, MI: Baker, 2001), 15.

3. John S. Tompkins, "Our Kindest City," *Reader's Digest* (July 1994), 55.

4. For a report from early in the outpouring, see Guy Chevreau, *Catch the Fire: The Toronto Blessing an Experience of Renewal and Revival* (New York: HarperCollins, 1995). For recent, retrospective reflections (and a vision for moving forward), see John and Carol Arnott, *Preparing for the Glory: Getting Ready for the Next Wave of Holy Spirit Outpouring* (Shippensburg, PA: Destiny Image, 2018).

CHAPTER 3

1. Michael Brown, "Equivocating or Evolving, President Obama Is Wrong Either Way," Townhall, May 12, 2012, https://townhall.com/columnists/michaelbrown/2012/05/12/equivocating_or_evolving_president_obama_is_wrong_either_way-n823824; see also Zeke J. Miller, "Axelrod: Obama Misled Nation When He Opposed Gay Marriage in 2008," *Time*, February 10, 2015, https://time.com/3702584/gay-marriage-axelrod-obama.

2. Gabriel Borelli, "About Six-in-Ten Americans Say Legalization of Same-Sex Marriage Is Good for Society," Pew Research Center, November 15, 2022, https://www.pewresearch.org/short-reads/2022/11/15/about-six-in-ten-americans-say-legalization-of-same-sex-marriage-is-good-for-society.

3. "Gay Rights in the 1960s," History, accessed November 13, 2023, https://www.history.com/topics/gay-rights/history-of-gay-rights#gay-rights-in-the-1960s.

4. Hugh Ryan, "How Dressing in Drag Was Labeled a Crime in the 20th Century," History, September 14, 2023, https://www.history.com/news/stonewall-riots-lgbtq-drag-three-article-rule.

5. Wikipedia, s.v. "New York City Drag March," accessed November 13, 2023, https://en.wikipedia.org/wiki/New_York_City_Drag_March.

6. "Libraries Respond: Drag Queen Story Hour," ALA, accessed November 13, 2023, https://www.ala.org/advocacy/libraries-respond-drag-queen-story-hour.

7. Associated Press, "NY Library Brings Drag Queens to Kids Story Hour," YouTube, May 16, 2017, https://www.youtube.com/watch?app=desktop&v=YOFkVZQ8etE&feature=youtu.be.

8. "Menstruating Men and the Latest Examples of Transanity," AskDrBrown, March 15, 2017, https://askdrbrown.org/article/menstruating-men-and-the-latest-examples-of-transanity.

9. "The Man Who Became a Woman Then a Dragon," The Line of Fire, YouTube, April 13, 2016, https://www.youtube.com/watch?app=desktop&v=q5-hq7wVOFc&feature=youtu.be; Michael Brown, "The Professor and Inventor Who Identifies as a Cheetah Named 'Spottacus,'" *Daily Wire*, November 13, 2023, https://www.dailywire.com/news/the-professor-and-inventor-who-identifies-as-a-cheetah-named-spottacus.

10. "Fact Sheet: Biden-Harris Administration Advances Equality and Visibility for Transgender Americans," The White House, March 31, 2022, https://www.whitehouse.gov/briefing-room/statements-releases/2022/03/31/fact-sheet-biden-harris-administration-advances-equality-and-visibility-for-transgender-americans.

11. "Christian Conservatives You Cannot Put Your Trust in Fox News," AskDrBrown, April 1, 2022, https://askdrbrown.org/article/christian-conservatives-you-cannot-put-your-trust-in.

12. John Corvino, "Homosexuality and the PIB Argument," *Ethics* 115, No. 3 (April 2005): 501–534, https://www.journals.uchicago.edu/doi/10.1086/428456.

13. Michael L. Brown, *A Queer Thing Happened to America: And What a Long Strange Trip It's Been* (Concord, NC: EqualTime Books, 2011), 50–51.

14. Linda Hirshman, *Victory: The Triumphant Gay Revolution* (New York: HarperCollins, 2012).

15. Hirshman, *Victory*, xiii.

16. Hirshman, *Victory*, xiii.

17. Andy Smith, "'Angels in America' Returns to Charlotte," *Charlotte Magazine*, April 21, 2014, https://www.charlottemagazine.com/angels-in-america-returns-to-charlotte.

18. Michael L. Brown, *Revolution in the Church* (Grand Rapids, MI: Chosen, 2002), 49–66.

19. Quoted in *New York Times*, April 22, 1959; see Chris Johnston, "'A Revolution Is Not a Bed of Roses': Fidel Castro in His Own Words," *The Guardian*, November 16, 2016, https://www.theguardian.com/world/2016/nov/26/a-revolution-is-not-a-bed-of-roses-fidel-castro-in-his-own-words.

20. Edmund Burke, "Nobody Made a Greater Mistake...," BrainyQuote, accessed November 13, 2023, https://www.brainyquote.com/quotes/edmund_burke_100421.

21. Marc Rubin, "GAA Must Be Restored to History," GayToday, accessed November 13, 2023, https://www.gaytoday.com/garchive/viewpoint/071999vi.htm.

22. Rubin, "GAA Must Be Restored to History."

23. Rubin, "GAA Must Be Restored to History."

24. Rubin, "GAA Must Be Restored to History."
25. The best-selling Christian book at that time was Hal Lindsey's *The Late Great Planet Earth*, originally published January 1, 1970.
26. Marshall Kirk and Erastes Pill, "The Overhauling of Straight America," Gay Homeland Foundation, accessed November 14, 2023, https://library.gayhomeland.org/0018/EN/EN_Overhauling_ Straight.htm.
27. Kirk and Pill, "The Overhauling of Straight America."
28. See Michael Knowles, *Speechless: Controlling Words, Controlling Minds* (Washington, DC: Regnery, 2021).

CHAPTER 4

1. Milton Quintanilla, "Report: Over 32,000 Babies' Lives Saved After Roe v. Wade Was Overturned," Christian Headlines, April 14, 2023, https://www.christianheadlines.com/contributors/milton-quintanilla/ report-over-32000-babies-lives-saved-after-roe-v-wade-was- overturned.html.
2. Piers Morgan, "'Where's My Straight Flag': Piers Morgan Clashes With LGBT Comedian," Sky News Australia, YouTube, June 15, 2023, https://www.youtube.com/watch?v=XoulC-h4yB4.
3. Much of the remainder of this chapter is drawn from an article I published called "The Cultural Tide Is Continuing to Turn, Just as Predicted," on The Line of Fire, June 21, 2023, https://thelineoffire. org/article/the-cultural-tide-is-continuing-to-turn-just-as-predicted.
4. Michael Brown, "2015: The Year of Pushback for Christians," Christian Post, January 6, 2015, https://www.christianpost.com/ news/2015-the-year-of-pushback-for-christians.html.
5. Will Potter, "California Woman, 18, Sues Doctors for Removing Her Breasts When She was Just Thirteen Because She Thought She Was Trans After Seeing Influencer Online," *Daily Mail*, June 17, 2023, https://www.dailymail.co.uk/news/article-12206847/Woman- pressured-breast-removal-13-erroneous-belief-transgender-lawsuit. html.
6. Allison Sullivan, "This Pride Month, Ordinary Americans Rise Against Extremes: A Rejection of Unchecked Gender Fluidity," MM Media, accessed January 2, 2024, https://www.msn.com/ en-us/news/us/this-pride-month-ordinary-americans-rise- against-extremes-a-rejection-of-unchecked-gender-fluidity/ ar-AA1coGUL?ocid=msedgntp&cvid=f6fc672c3bf4440cac4ac3c 7936e1512&ei=18.
7. "Does 2023 Bring the Great Pushback Against LGBTQ+ Rights?," Edge Media Network, May 22, 2023, https://newsroom.lmu.edu/

lmu-in-the-news/does-2023-bring-the-great-pushback-against-lgbtq-rights.

8. Spencer Lindquist, "American Support for Same Sex Relations Dropped Seven Points Since Last Year," The Daily Wire, June 16, 2023, https://www.dailywire.com/news/american-support-for-same-sex-relations-dropped-seven-points-since-last-year.

9. James Lynch, "The Left's Mass Deception About Gender Is Completely Failing, Major New Study Reveals," Daily Caller, accessed January 2, 2024, https://www.msn.com/en-us/news/opinion/the-left-s-mass-deception-about-gender-is-completely-failing-major-new-study-reveals/ar-AA1cjap3?ocid=msedgntp&cvid=613a219c68354a8bba0d972fdda01b58&ei=13.

10. Dave Urbanski, "Parents Livid Over Pride Video Shown to 3rd, 4th, 5th Grades…," Blaze Media, June 7, 2023, https://www.theblaze.com/news/parents-livid-over-pride-video-shown-to-3rd-4th-5th-graders-in-which-child-says-i-never-really-felt-like-a-boy-and-i-dont-really-feel-like-a-girl-so-id-rather-be-both.

11. "'My Pronouns Are USA': Massachusetts Middle School Tries to Make Children Wear Rainbow Clothing for Pride…," Post Millennial, June 13, 2023, https://thepostmillennial.com/my-pronouns-are-usa-massachusetts-middle-school-pride-revolt.

12. Ingrid Jacques, "Social Conservatism Is on the Rise. Maybe DeSantis Is on to Something With Anti-'Woke' Fight," USA Today, June 15, 2023, https://www.usatoday.com/story/opinion/columnist/2023/06/15/americans-more-conservative-liberal-social-issues/70320558007/.

13. Sarah Parshall Perry, "The Uprising: Families Clash With Schools Over LGBTQ Propaganda," Daily Signal, June 16, 2023, https://www.dailysignal.com/2023/06/16/the-uprising-families-clash-with-schools-over-lgbtq-propaganda/.

14. Ace Vincent, "Uh-Oh! Pride Parades Get Thumbs Down From Americans: Is It Too Much Rainbow for Business?," Stock Dork, June 12, 2023, https://www.thestockdork.com/uh-oh-pride-parades-get-thumbs-down-from-americans-is-it-too-much-rainbow-for-business/.

15. Carl Smith, "Storm Clouds Gathering Over Pride Month," Governing, June 8, 2023, https://www.governing.com/health/storm-clouds-are-gathering-over-pride-month.

16. Ben Appel, "It's a Shame What Pride Has Become," Washington Examiner, accessed January 3, 2024, https://www.msn.com/en-us/news/us/it-s-a-shame-what-pride-has-become/ar-AA1cCHKK?ocid=msedgntp&cvid=cf809d9fef974aeda344e2e97def29f6&ei=10.

17. Kevin Harrish, "World Reacts as Transgender Athletes Are Losing Support in America," Next Impulse Sports, accessed January 3, 2024, https://www.msn.com/en-us/news/us/world-reacts-as-transgender-athletes-are-losing-support-in-america/ar-AA1cuecH?ocid=msedgntp&cvid=0f695a7716374105 89861c77e038497c&ei=14.

18. Associated Press, "City Officially Bans 'Pride' Flags From Public Property, Tells LGBT Objectors 'You're Already Represented,'" The Western Journal, June 14, 2023, https://www.westernjournal.com/ap-detroit-area-city-bans-lgbtq-pride-flags-public-property.

19. Perry, "The Uprising: Families Clash With Schools Over LGBTQ Propaganda."

20. Jeffrey M. Jones, "Social Conservatism in U.S. Highest in About a Decade," Gallup, June 8, 2023, https://news.gallup.com/poll/506765/social-conservatism-highest-decade.aspx.

21. Jeffrey M. Jones, "Fewer in U.S. Say Same-Sex Relations Morally Acceptable," Gallup, June 16, 2023, https://news.gallup.com/poll/507230/fewer-say-sex-relations-morally-acceptable.aspx?utm_source=alert&utm_medium=email&utm_content=morelink&utm_campaign=syndication.

22. "National State of Emergency for LGBTQ+ Americans," Human Rights Campaign, accessed January 3, 2024, https://www.hrc.org/campaigns/national-state-of-emergency-for-lgbtq-americans.

23. Dr. Michael Brown, "The Human Side of LGBTQ Pride and the Predicament It Causes for Loving Christians," The Line of Fire, June 5, 2023, https://askdrbrown.org/article/the-human-side-of-lgbtq-pride-and-the-predicament-it-causes-for-loving-christians.

24. Michael L. Brown, PhD, *Outlasting the Gay Revolution* (Washington, DC: WND Books, 2015), 37.

25. Brown, "The Cultural Tide Is Continuing to Turn, Just as Predicted."

26. Chadwick Moore, "Why LGBTs Are Running Out of Pride," *New York Post*, accessed January 3, 2024, https://www.msn.com/en-us/news/politics/why-lgbts-are-running-out-of-pride/ar-AA1cnt1X?ocid=msedgntp&cvid=bd46cf7cf32342fdb37 376725dbb4de6&ei=18.

27. Dr. Michael Brown, "Why You Cannot Separate the T (or Q) From the LGB," The Line of Fire, May 23, 2023, https://askdrbrown.org/article/why-you-cannot-separate-the-t-or-q-from-the-lgb.

28. Sullivan, "This Pride Month, Ordinary Americans Rise Against Extremes."

29. Fox News, "Joe Rogan Says Customers Have Had 'Enough' of Woke Messaging: 'Stop Shoving This Down Everybody's Throat,'" *New York Post*, accessed January 3, 2024, https://www.msn.com/en-us/

money/companies/joe-rogan-says-customers-have-had-enough-of-woke-messaging-stop-shoving-this-down-everybody-s-throat/ar-AA1cnqWZ.

30. Gabriel Hays, "Richard Dawkins Declares There Are Only Two Sexes as Matter of Science: 'That's All There Is to It,'" Fox News, March 21, 2023, https://www.foxnews.com/media/richard-dawkins-declares-only-two-sexes-matter-science-thats-all; Bill Maher, "If the Spike in Trans Kids Is Natural, Why Is it Regional?" HBO on Real Clear Politics, May 23, 2022, https:// www.realclearpolitics.com/video/2022/05/22/bill_maher_on_trans_kids_were_literally_experimenting_on_children_weighing_trade-offs_is_not_bigotry.html; Dan Bernstein, "Martina Navratilova Weighs in Again on Transgender Athletes After College Record Broken," Daily Express US, accessed January 3, 2024, https://www.msn.com/en-us/sports/tennis/martina-navratilova-weighs-in-again-on-transgender-athletes-after-college-record-broken/ar-AA1kogUU; Olivia Petter, "JK Rowling Criticized Over 'Transphobic' Tweet About Menstruation," The Independent, June 15, 2020, https://www.independent.co.uk/life-style/jk-rowling-tweet-women-menstruate-people-transphobia-twitter-a9552866.html. See also Michael Brown, "7 Times the Left Ate Their Own," The Daily Wire, accessed January 3, 2024, https://www.dailywire.com/news/7-times-the-left-ate-their-own.

31. See Michael L. Brown, *The Silencing of the Lambs: The Ominous Rise of Cancel Culture and How We Can Overcome It* (Lake Mary, FL: Frontline, 2022); Joseph A. Wulfsohn, "Bill Maher's Warning to the Left: Cancel Culture Is 'Real' and 'Coming to a Neighborhood Near You,'" Fox News, February 27, 2021, https://www.foxnews.com/entertainment/bill-maher-cancel-culture-gina-carano-chris-harrison; Tyler McCarthy, "Miley Cyrus Offers to Educate DaBaby Amid Scandal, Rails Against 'Cancel Culture' in Social Media Post," Fox News, August 5, 2021, https://www.foxnews.com/entertainment/miley-cyrus-dababy-scandal-cancel-culture-social-media; Georgia Slater, "Sharon Stone Calls Cancel Culture the 'Stupidest Thing I Have Ever Seen': 'Give People an Opportunity,'" *People*, March 26, 2021, https://people.com/movies/sharon-stone-calls-cancel-culture-stupidest-thing-ive-ever-seen; Chloe Melas, "Kelly Osbourne Speaks Out About 'Cancel Culture,'" CNN Entertainment, April 29, 2021, https://www.cnn.com/2021/04/29/entertainment/kelly-osbourne-sharon-osbourne-the-talk-interview/index.html.

CHAPTER 5

1. S. D. Gordon, "Prayer Is Striking the Winning Blow...," AZQuotes, accessed November 14, 2023, https://www.azquotes.com/quote/1124867.
2. "Derek Prince Quotes," Derek Prince Ministries, accessed November 14, 2023, https://www.derekprince.com/about/quotes.
3. See Brown, *The Silencing of the Lambs*, 135–140.
4. Larry Tomczak, "Four Years in Seminary or Four Minutes in Hell?," Charisma News, August 10, 2023, https://www.charismanews.com/opinion/heres-the-deal/93013-4-years-in-seminary-or-4-minutes-in-hell.
5. "Hudson Taylor Quotes," AZQuotes, accessed November 15, 2023, https://www.azquotes.com/author/17456-Hudson_Taylor.
6. Galen B. Royer, "David Livingstone: Africa's Great Missionary and Explorer," Wholesome Words Home, accessed November 15, 2023, https://www.wholesomewords.org/missions/bliving2.html.
7. Source unknown.
8. Cited in Michael L. Brown, *It's Time to Rock the Boat: A Call to God's People to Rise Up and Preach a Confrontational Gospel* (Shippensburg, PA: Destiny Image, 1993), 178.
9. Joe Oden, *Prayer That Ignites Revivals* (Grand Rapids: Chosen, 2024). Joe came to faith as a direct result of the Brownsville Revival and graduated from our ministry school.

CHAPTER 6

1. See also 1 Peter 2:12.
2. Tim Keller, "5 Features That Made the Early Church Unique," TGC, January 10, 2020, https://www.thegospelcoalition.org/article/5-features-early-church-unique.
3. J. W. Provonsha, MD, cited in Michael L. Brown, *Israel's Divine Healer* (Grand Rapids, MI: Zondervan, 1995), 66. Provonsha contends that the Hellenistic body-soul dichotomy that strongly influenced the post–New Testament church brought about a decreased emphasis on the importance of ministry to one's physical needs, noting also that "the Post-Apostolic Church often saw the healing ministry of Jesus, and that [it was] committed to the Church, as radically opposed to the methodology of 'pagan' physicians of the period. It was miracle against scientific method—Christ's healings were miraculous, not scientific! But the early Church often failed to distinguish between 'miracle' and 'magic.'" See Brown, *Israel's Divine Healer*, 66.
4. Cited in Brown, *Israel's Divine Healer*, 66.

5. See *The Proceedings of the Consultation on the Study Program of Healing Ministry, October 30–November 1, 1980* (Seoul: Asian Center for Theological Studies and Mission/Korea Christian Medico-Evangelical Association, n.d.), 3, 5. For further discussion, see Brown, *Israel's Divine Healer*, 63–66.

6. See 1 John 4:7–21.

7. Gary Ferngren, "'Honour the Image of God': The Incarnation and Early Christian Philanthropy," ABC, July 15, 2014, https://www.abc.net.au/religion/honour-the-image-of-god-the-incarnation-and-early-christian-phil/10099186. This lengthy article was referenced in Keller's article cited previously, "5 Features That Made the Early Church Unique."

8. Ferngren, "Honour the Image of God."

9. Wikipedia, s.v. "Hamas," accessed November 30, 2023, https://en.wikipedia.org/wiki/Hamas#Social_services_wing.

10. Tompkins, "Our Kindest City."

11. Francis A. Schaeffer, *The Complete Works of Francis A. Schaeffer: A Christian Worldview* (Westchester, IL: Crossway Books, 1982), 4:88.

12. Schaeffer, *The Complete Works of Francis A. Schaeffer*, 4:89.

13. Schaeffer, *The Complete Works of Francis A. Schaeffer*, 4:92.

CHAPTER 7

1. Michael Lipka and Conrad Hackett, "Why Muslims Are the World's Fastest-Growing Religious Group," Pew Research Center, April 6, 2017, https://www.pewresearch.org/short-reads/2017/04/06/why-muslims-are-the-worlds-fastest-growing-religious-group.

2. Claire Porter Robbins, "How Israeli Youth Helped Usher in the Farthest Right-Wing Government Ever," Vox, February 23, 2023, https://www.vox.com/world-politics/2023/2/23/23609584/israel-right-wing-young-voters-palestine.

3. Amy Hawkins, "Marriages in China Drop to Record Low Despite Government Push," *The Guardian*, June 13, 2023, https://www.theguardian.com/world/2023/jun/14/marriages-in-china-drop-to-record-low-despite-government-push.

4. "10 Causes of High Birth Rate in India—Explained!," Economics Discussion, accessed November 20, 2023, https://www.economicsdiscussion.net/articles/10-causes-of-high-birth-rate-in-india-explained/2243.

5. Dr. Michael L. Brown (@DrMichaelLBrown), "In your opinion, what is the #1 most prized value in America, the one thing we cherish the most?," X (formerly Twitter), June 27, 2023, https://twitter.com/DrMichaelLBrown/status/1670225453448155136.

6. "Why Is the Family So Important to Muslims?," Discover Islam, accessed November 20, 2023, https://www.discoverislam.com/why-is-the-family-so-important-to-muslims#.

7. "Large Families," The Jewish Woman, accessed November 20, 2023, https://www.chabad.org/theJewishWoman/article_cdo/aid/4623747/jewish/Large-Families.htm#.

8. Maimonides, "Laws of Marriage," *Mishneh Torah*, 15:16.

9. "Will Your Grandchild Be Jewish?," Simple to Remember, accessed November 20, 2023, https://www.simpletoremember.com/vitals/images/Will_Your_Grandchild_Be_Jewish_Chart.jpg. Used with permission.

10. Conclusion: With the exception of the Orthodox, the chances of American Jews having Jewish grandchildren and great-grandchildren are becoming increasingly remote based on the following: (1) intermarriage rates; (2) the increasing percentage of Jews who do not marry and/or marry but choose to not have children; (3) 2018 Orthodox Jewish day school attendance: 261,416; Reform/Conservative Jewish day school attendance: 10,930.

    This chart is part of an article coauthored by Richard M. Horowitz and Antony Gordon titled "Will Your Grandchild Be Jewish? 2021 Update." The article is based on the raw data of the most recent national demographic studies on American Jewry conducted by the Pew Research Center and released on October 1, 2013, and May 11, 2021, and the Avi Chai Foundation, 2020. For reprint permission, contact Antony Gordon at 323-314-1898 or antony.gordon@stealthcm.com, richardmhorowitz@gmail.com.

11. Miska Salemann, "Birth Rates Are the Right's Secret Weapon as Liberal Values Backfire," The Western Journal, July 24, 2021, https://www.westernjournal.com/birth-rates-rights-secret-weapon-liberal-values-backfire.

12. Salemann, "Birth Rates Are the Right's Secret Weapon..."

13. Ryan Burge, "The Future of American Religion: Birth Rates Show Who's Having More Kids," Religion Unplugged, October 4, 2021, https://religionunplugged.com/news/2021/10/4/the-future-of-american-religion-birth-rates-show-whos-having-more-kids.

14. Joshua A. Krisch, "Republicans Have More Kids Than Democrats. A Lot More Kids," Fatherly, July 8, 2022, https://www.fatherly.com/health/republicans-have-more-children; see also Michael Brown, "New Poll Finds Conservatives Happier Than Liberals, Marriage and Family Strong Predictors," The Daily Wire, https://www.dailywire.com/news/new-poll-finds-conservatives-happier-than-liberals-marriage-and-family-strong-predictors.

15. Lyman Stone, "America's Growing Religious-Secular Fertility Divide," Institute for Family Studies, August 8, 2022, https://ifstudies.org/blog/americas-growing-religious-secular-fertility-divide.
16. We removed the comment but kept a screen shot.
17. "Chapter 3: Demographic Profiles in Religious Groups," Pew Research Center, May 12, 2015, https://www.pewresearch.org/religion/2015/05/12/chapter-3-demographic-profiles-of-religious-groups.
18. Stone, "America's Growing Religious-Secular Fertility Divide."
19. Stone, "America's Growing Religious-Secular Fertility Divide."
20. I'm aware that many sincere Christians believe that every couple should simply trust God to open and close the womb, resulting in as many (or few) babies as He desires for each family. With respect to their convictions, that is not my own position.
21. For the powerful Christian role in adoption, see, for example, https://christianadoptions.org.
22. Stone, "America's Growing Religious-Secular Fertility Divide."
23. Matt Walsh, "TikTok Is Making Mental Illness Trendy," YouTube, accessed November 21, 2023, https://www.youtube.com/watch?v=2d6azjXMhSA.
24. Potter, "California Woman, 18, Sues Doctors…"
25. Ginsberg/Podhoretz, "The Allen Ginsberg Project," Allen Ginsberg Project, February 14, 2016, https://allenginsberg.org/2016/02/ginsbergpodhoretz.
26. William Ayers, "The Real Bill Ayers," *New York Times*, December 5, 2008, https://www.nytimes.com/2008/12/06/opinion/06ayers.html?_r=2.
27. Bernie Quigley, "Obama and Bill Ayers: Together From the Beginning," *The Hill*, September 24, 2008, https://thehill.com/blogs/pundits-blog/presidential-campaign/28339-obama-and-bill-ayers-together-from-the-beginning.
28. Quigley, "Obama and Bill Ayers."
29. John Sinclair, "White Panther Statement," 1968, quoted in John Strausbaugh, *Rock Til You Drop: The Decline From Rebellion to Nostalgia* (London: Verso, 2001), 89; for additional relevant quotes and anecdotes, see Michael L. Brown, *The Power of Music: God's Call to Change the World One Song at a Time* (Lake Mary, FL: Charisma House, 2018).
30. Cited in Brown, *A Queer Thing Happened to America*, 84.
31. Karista Baldwin, "Watch: Drag Queen Admits They're 'Grooming' Your Kids During Story Hour," The Western Journal, November 30,

2018, https://www.westernjournal.com/watch-drag-queen-admits-grooming-kids-story-hour.

32. Dan MacGuill, "Did a Convicted Sex Offender Read to Children at a Houston Public Library?," Snopes, October 7, 2019, https://www.snopes.com/fact-check/drag-queen-library-convicted.

CHAPTER 8

1. "Derek Prince Quotes," Derek Prince Ministries, accessed November 21, 2023, https://www.derekprince.com/en-us/about/quotes.

2. W. Bradford Wilcox, "The Evolution of Divorce," National Affairs, Fall 2009, https://nationalaffairs.com/publications/detail/the-evolution-of-divorce.

3. Judy Parejko, "The 40th Anniversary of 'No-Fault' Divorce," Catholic Exchange, September 5, 2009, https://catholicexchange.com/the-40th-anniversary-of-%E2%80%9Cno-fault%E2%80%9D-divorce.

4. Kevin B. Skinner, PhD, "Is Porn Really Destroying 500,000 Marriages Annually?," Psychology Today, December 12, 2011, https://www.psychologytoday.com/us/blog/inside-porn-addiction/201112/is-porn-really-destroying-500000-marriages-annually.

5. David Shultz, "Divorce Rates Double When People Start Watching Porn," Science, August 26, 2016, https://www.science.org/content/article/divorce-rates-double-when-people-start-watching-porn.

6. "Study: Watching Pornography Can Lead to Divorce," EndAllDisease.com, accessed November 21, 2023, https://www.endalldisease.com/study-watching-pornography-can-lead-to-divorce.

7. John Stonestreet and Maria Baer, "Healthy Cultures Rest on Dads' Shoulders," The Stream, June 17, 2023, https://stream.org/healthy-cultures-rest-on-dads-shoulders.

8. Nancy Pearcey, The Toxic War on Masculinity: How Christianity Reconciles the Sexes (Grand Rapids: Baker Books, 2023), 36–37.

9. Pearcey, The Toxic War on Masculinity, 36–37.

10. Pearcey, The Toxic War on Masculinity, 36–37.

11. Brad Wilcox, cited in Pearcey, The Toxic War on Masculinity, 41-42.

12. Pearcey also cited Clay Routledge, "Religious Faith and the Family: An Interview with Dr. W. Bradford Wilcox," Quillette, May 23, 2019, https://quillette.com/2019/05/23/religious-faith-and-the-family-an-interview-with-dr-w-bradford-wilcox/; W. Bradford Wilcox and Steven L. Nock, "What's Love Got to Do With It? Equality, Equity, Commitment and Women's Marital Quality," Social Forces 84, no. 3 (March 2006): 1340, https://psycnet.apa.org/record/2006-04089-001; W. Bradford Wilcox, Jason S. Carroll, and Laurie DeRose, "Religious Men Can Be Devoted Dads, Too," New York Times, May 18, 2019, https://www.nytimes.com/2019/05/18/

opinion/sunday/happy-marriages.html; W. Bradford Wilcox, "Soft Patriarchs: A Conversation With Brad Wilcox," interview by Michael Cromartie, *Books & Culture*, September/October 2004, https://www.booksandculture.com/articles/2004/sepoct/7.20.html; W. Bradford Wilcox, "Affectionate Patriarchs: An Interview With W. Bradford Wilcox," interview by Douglas LeBlanc, *Christianity Today*, August 1, 2004, https://www.christianitytoday.com/ct/2004/august/26.44.html; W. Bradford Wilcox, "Faith and Marriage, Better Together?," *Principles*, 3, no. 3, Christendom College, accessed February 20, 2024, https://www.getprinciples.com/faith-and-marriage-better-together/.

13. Here Pearcey cited Elizabeth E. Brusco, *The Reformation of Machismo: Evangelical Conversion and Gender in Colombia* (Austin, TX: University of Texas Press, 1995), 3, 9, 6, 137; Sara Miller Llana, "In Colombia, Women Use New Faith to Gain Equality," *Christian Science Monitor*, December 19, 2007, https://www.csmonitor.com/2007/1219/p01s03-woam.html; Bernice Martin, "The Pentecostal Gender Paradox" in *The Blackwell Companion to Sociology of Religion*, ed. Richard K. Fenn (Malden, MA: Blackwell, 2001, 2003), 54; Nicholas Kristof and Sheryl WuDunn, *Half the Sky: Turning Oppression Into Opportunity for Women Worldwide* (New York: Random House, 2009), 143.

14. Brown, *Saving a Sick America*, 81–102; Brown, *Outlasting the Gay Revolution*, 189–217.

15. Megan Brock and Laurel Duggan, "Minnesota's New 'LGBT Education Specialist' Thinks Teachers Should 'Explain Nonbinary Identities' to Preschoolers," MSN, accessed November 21, 2023, https://www.msn.com/en-us/news/us/minnesotas-new-lgbt-education-specialist-thinks-teachers-should-explain-nonbinary-identities-to-preschoolers/ar-AA1cGhoL.

16. It was first published in 1989. See Leslea Newman and Laura Cornell, *Heather Has Two Mommies* (Somerville, MA: Candlewick Press, 2015).

17. David Ng, "DC Comics Pushes Gay Pride on Children With Same-Sex Superhero Couple 'Midnighter and Apollo,'" Breitbart, June 17, 2023, https://www.breitbart.com/entertainment/2023/06/17/dc-comics-pushes-gay-pride-on-children-with-same-sex-superhero-couple-midnighter-and-apollo.

18. It was first published in Dutch in 2000. See Linda de Haan and Stern Nijland, *King and King* (Berkeley, CA: Tricycle Press, 2003).

19. Jeff Johnston, "Focus on the Family Education Resources," Daily Citizen, May 22, 2020, https://dailycitizen.focusonthefamily.com/focus-on-the-family-education-resources.

20. See, for example, Jason Jimenez, *Parenting Gen Z: Guiding Your Child Through a Hostile Culture* (Colorado Springs, CO: Focus on the Family, 2023); Tom Gilson, *Critical Conversations: A Christian Parents' Guide to Discussing Homosexuality With Teens* (Grand Rapids, MI: Kregel, 2016).

21. See, for example, James Emery White, *Meet Generation Z: Understanding and Reaching the New Post-Christian World* (Grand Rapids, MI: Baker Books, 2017); David Kinnaman and Mark Mattlock, *Faith for Exiles: 5 Ways for a New Generation to Follow Jesus in Digital Babylon* (Grand Rapids, MI: Baker Books, 2019).

22. See, for example, teachthemdiligently.net and answersingenesis.org/homeschool-edition. For personalized support for a wide range of homeschoolers (from all faith and political backgrounds), designed by a homeschool teenager, see https://standtogether.org/news/canary-academy-providing-homeschool-resources-for-learning/.

23. Interestingly, when I searched online to see who said, "You teach what you know but you reproduce who you are," one of the first links that came up was the Christian-based teachthemdiligently.net website, which featured this very quote. How interesting! It provides "Resources and Experiences to Strengthen Christian Homeschool Families."

24. You can listen to our interview here: https://askdrbrown.org/video/ron-luce-talks-with-dr.-brown-on-how-to-keep-young; for his website with resources for churches, go here: https://generationnext.me/what-is-project-13.

25. See https://g2gmandate.com/Articles/13030/Meet_The_Team.aspx.

26. Elon Musk (@ElonMusk), "The childless have little stake in the future," X (formerly Twitter), July 1, 2023, https://twitter.com/elonmusk/status/1675206140848746496.

27. Motoko Rich and Makiko Inoue, "A New Source of Fuel in an Aging Japan: Adult Incontinence," *New York Times*, November 15, 2021, https://www.nytimes.com/2021/11/15/world/asia/adult-diapers-japan.html.

28. Mark Steyn, *America Alone: The End of the World as We Know It* (Washington, DC: Regnery Books, 2006).

29. Chiara Albanese et al., "Musk Warns of Italy's Shrinking Population at Meloni Event," Bloomberg, accessed January 8, 2024, https://www.msn.com/en-us/money/other/musk-warns-of-italy-s-shrinking-population-at-meloni-event/ar-AA1lAUOL.

30. Giulio Meotti, "Europe's Childless Leaders Sleepwalking Us to Disaster," Gatestone Institute, May 6, 2017, https://www.gatestoneinstitute.org/10306/childless-europe. In 2018 Snopes pushed back against this claim. Still, they agreed that it is true

that "several high-profile European leaders do not have biological children," while also noting that "a majority of European leaders have biological children of their own, and others have stepchildren from their spouses' previous marriages." See Alex Kasprak, "Is Europe Governed by 'Childless Baby Boomers'?," Snopes, November 28, 2018, https://www.snopes.com/fact-check/europe-childless-leaders.

CHAPTER 9

1. "An Outline History of Religion in American Schools (No Bible/Prayer in Public Schools? Show Me)," Free Republic, March 8, 2009, https://freerepublic.com/focus/religion/2201818/posts.
2. Brown, *Saving a Sick America*, 24–26.
3. Brown, *Saving a Sick America*, 20–23.
4. Brown, *Saving a Sick America*, 17–18.
5. Patricia Nell Warren, "Future Shock," *The Advocate*, Oct 3, 1995.
6. Jon A. Shields, "The Disappearing Conservative Professor," National Affairs, fall 2018, https://nationalaffairs.com/publications/detail/the-disappearing-conservative-professor.
7. John Gage, "Harvard Newspaper Survey Finds 1% of Faculty Members Identify as Conservative," *Washington Examiner*, March 4, 2020, https://www.washingtonexaminer.com/news/harvard-newspaper-survey-finds-1-of-faculty-members-identify-as-conservative. For an individual professor's perspective, see Jerry Bergman, PhD, "Ratio of Liberal to Conservative Professors Has Profoundly Changed," KPC News, October 10, 2019, https://www.kpcnews.com/opinions/article_72a36307-576f-517e-8a43-64eb7f024e27.html.
8. Brown, *The Silencing of the Lambs*, 18.
9. Michael Brown, "A Liberal Professor Admits to the Leftist Takeover of America," The Stream, January 3, 2023, https://stream.org/a-liberal-professor-admits-to-the-leftist-takeover-of-america.
10. Cited in Brown, "A Liberal Professor Admits to the Leftist Takeover of America."
11. See Brown, *A Queer Thing Happened to America*, 88.
12. See Brown, *A Queer Thing Happened to America*, 96.
13. Aaron Life, "Almost Half of Elite University's Students Identify as LGBT," Daily Caller, July 10, 2023, https://dailycaller.com/2023/07/10/half-of-brown-students-are-lgbt.
14. Michael Brown, "Sociological Contagion and the Growing Non-Binary Movement," The Daily Wire, accessed November 27, 2023, https://www.dailywire.com/news/sociological-contagion-and-the-growing-non-binary-movement.

15. Lexi Lonas, "1 in 4 High School Students Identifies as LGBTQ," *The Hill*, April 27, 2023, https://thehill.com/homenews/education/3975959-one-in-four-high-school-students-identify-as-lgbtq.

16. Amelia Gentleman, "'An Explosion': What Is Behind the Rise in Girls Questioning Their Gender Identity?," *The Guardian*, November 24, 2022, https://www.theguardian.com/society/2022/nov/24/an-explosion-what-is-behind-the-rise-in-girls-questioning-their-gender-identity.

17. Jack Montgomery, "Not Safe: UK Health Service Shuts Down Tavistock, Infamous for Child Trans Treatments," Breitbart, July 29, 2022, https://www.breitbart.com/europe/2022/07/29/not-safe-uk-health-service-shuts-down-tavistock-infamous-for-child-trans-treatments.

18. "NEA LGBTQ+ Resources," NEA, June 2021, https://www.nea.org/resource-library/nea-lgbtq-resources.

19. Gage Klipper, "The Source of the Marxist Takeover of American Institutions Is So Obvious It Hurts," Daily Caller, June 2, 2023, https://dailycaller.com/2023/06/02/source-marxist-takeover-american-institutions-obvious-hurts.

20. Bobby Harrington, "The Long March Through the Institutions of Society," Renew.org, accessed November 27, 2023, https://renew.org/the-long-march-through-the-institutions-of-society.

21. Jonathan Turley (@JonathanTurley), "Nationally, less than a third of Americans identify as 'liberal'...," X (formerly Twitter), June 1, 2023, https://twitter.com/JonathanTurley/status/1664230829449461761.

22. "Harvard Survey: Over 75 Percent of the Harvard Faculty Identifies as 'Liberal' or 'Very Liberal,'" Jonathan Turley, June 1, 2023, https://jonathanturley.org/2023/06/01/harvard-survey-over-75-percent-of-the-harvard-faculty-identifies-as-liberal-or-very-liberal.

23. Eric Kaufmann, "We Have the Data to Prove It: Universities Are Discriminating Against Conservatives," *Newsweek*, March 3, 2021, https://www.newsweek.com/we-have-data-prove-it-universities-are-hostile-conservatives-opinion-1573551; see also Douglas MacKinnon, "The Appalling Discrimination Against America's Young Conservatives," *The Hill*, November 9, 2019, https://thehill.com/opinion/campaign/469261-the-appalling-discrimination-against-americas-young-conservatives. For specific examples, see my book *The Silencing of the Lambs*.

24. Alex Nester, "Majority of Academics Support Discriminating Against Conservatives, Study Shows," *Washington Free Beacon*, March 2, 2021, https://freebeacon.com/campus/majority-of-academics-support-discriminating-against-conservatives-study-shows.

25. According to the *Washington Free Beacon* article, "Seventy percent of conservative academics reported that their department created a hostile environment for conservative ideas, according to the study. Nine in 10 Trump-supporting academics reported that they would not feel comfortable expressing their views to a colleague. And more than half of conservative academics surveyed admitted to self-censoring their research and teaching."

26. Rufo, America's Cultural Revolution, 4.

27. Brown, *Saving a Sick America*, 109–110.

28. Rebecca Devitt, "What Countries Is Homeschooling Illegal and Legal?," How Do I Homeschool?, January 31, 2023, https://howdoihomeschool.com/homeschool-legal-illegal.

29. "Our History," HSLDA, accessed November 27, 2023, https://web.archive.org/web/20180407232148/https:/hslda.org/about/history.asp.

30. For a relevant 2017 article, see Jeremiah Poff, "Homeschool Students Still Face Bias in College Admissions, Even When They Meet Requirements," The College Fix, August 8, 2017, https://www.thecollegefix.com/homeschooled-students-still-face-bias-college-admissions-even-meet-requirements. See also Daniel Beasley, Esq., "Law Helps Reverse College Rejection of Homeschool Grad," HSLDA, November 16, 2020, https://hslda.org/post/law-helps-reverse-college-rejection-of-homeschool-grad.

31. Brian D. Ray, PhD, "Research Facts on Homeschooling," NHERI, July 20, 2023, https://www.nheri.org/research-facts-on-homeschooling.

32. Cara Goodwin, PhD, "The Research on Homeschooling," *Psychology Today*, September 1, 2021, https://www.psychologytoday.com/us/blog/parenting-translator/202109/the-research-homeschooling.

33. Goodwin, "The Research on Homeschooling"; see further, Liz Hurley, "Benefits of Homeschooling," Learnopoly, accessed November 27, 2023, https://learnopoly.com/benefits-of-homeschooling.

34. Michael Brown, "Canada's Supreme Court Rules Against the Bible," Townhall, June 16, 2018, https://townhall.com/columnists/michaelbrown/2018/06/16/canadas-supreme-court-rules-against-the-bible-n2491315. See also, Kathleen Harris, "Trinity Western Loses Fight for Christian Law School as Court Rules Limits on Religious Freedom 'Reasonable,'" CBC, June 15, 2018, https://www.cbc.ca/news/politics/trinity-western-supreme-court-decision-1.4707240.

35. Deborah Gyapong, "Trinity Western University Removes Mandatory Community Covenant," *Catholic Register*, August 14, 2018, https://www.catholicregister.org/

item/27821-trinity-western-university-removes-mandatory-community-covenant.

36. Wikipedia, s.v. "Boston University," accessed November 28, 2023, https://en.wikipedia.org/wiki/Boston_University.

37. "Past Presidents," Yale University, accessed November 28, 2023, https://president.yale.edu/about/past-presidents.

38. Katherine Hamilton, "American Library Association President Stands by Tweet Admitting She Is a 'Marxist Lesbian,' States Look to Cut Ties," Breitbart, accessed February 16, 2024, https://www.breitbart.com/politics/2023/08/08/american-library-association-president-stands-tweet-admitting-she-marxist-lesbian-states-look-cut-ties.

39. Text messages, July 21, 2023, used with permission.

40. Text from Katie W., August 1, 2023, used with permission.

CHAPTER 10

1. "Jesus Film Project Ministry Statistics," Jesus Film Project, accessed November 28, 2023, https://www.jesusfilm.org/partners/resources/strategies/statistics.

2. "ADF at the Supreme Court," Alliance Defending Freedom, accessed November 28, 2023, https://adflegal.org/us-supreme-court-wins.

3. "Dr. Bill Bright," Alliance Defending Freedom, accessed November 28, 2023, https://adflegal.org/profile/dr-bill-bright.

4. "ADF at the Supreme Court," Alliance Defending Freedom.

5. "SCOTUS Rules 9-0 in Favor of Christian Flag Case," Liberty Counsel, May 2, 2022, https://lc.org/newsroom/details/050222-scotus-rules-in-favor-of-christian-flag-case-1.

6. Tony Kinnett, "Breaking: California Bill Would Charge Any Parent Who Doesn't Affirm Transgenderism With 'Child Abuse,'" Daily Signal, June 9, 2023, https://www.dailysignal.com/2023/06/09/california-bill-would-charge-any-parent-doesnt-affirm-transgenderism-child-abuse.

7. "Equality Maps: Conversion Therapy Laws," Movement Advancement Project, accessed January 9, 2024, https://www.lgbtmap.org/equality-maps/conversion_therapy.

8. Michael Brown, "California's Shocking 'You Must Stay Gay' Bill," The Stream, April 5, 2018, https://stream.org/californias-shocking-must-stay-gay-bill.

9. Jeff Johnston, "Canadian Dad Sentenced for Trying to Protect Daughter From Transgender Medical Procedures," Daily Citizen, April 20, 2021, https://dailycitizen.focusonthefamily.com/canadian-dad-sentenced-for-trying-to-protect-daughter-from-transgender-medical-procedures; Michael Brown, "A Word of Encouragement

From a Courageous Canadian Parliamentarian," The Stream, May 13, 2021, https://stream.org/a-word-of-encouragement-from-a-courageous-canadian-parliamentarian; Kinnett, "Breaking: California Bill Would Charge Any Parent Who Doesn't Affirm Transgenderism With 'Child Abuse'"; for another chilling incident, see Tyler O'Neil, "Christian Facing Prosecution for Giving Testimony Warns: Authorities Target 'Any Dissenting Opinion' on LGBT Issues," Daily Signal, January 23, 2023, https://www.dailysignal.com/2023/01/23/christian-charity-worker-in-malta-prosecuted-for-sharing-his-personal-testimony-about-rejecting-homosexual-activity.

10. For updates, see here: "Tracking Abortion Bans Across the Country," *New York Times*, accessed November 28, 2023, https://www.nytimes.com/interactive/2022/us/abortion-laws-roe-v-wade.html.

11. Jordan Boyd, "Momentum From *Dobbs* Led Legislatures All Around the Country to Pass Popular Pro-Life Laws," The Federalist, May 24, 2023, https://thefederalist.com/2023/05/24/momentum-from-dobbs-led-legislatures-all-around-the-country-to-pass-popular-pro-life-laws.

12. "National State of Emergency for LGBTQ+ Americans," Human Rights Campaign, accessed November 28, 2023, https://www.hrc.org/campaigns/national-state-of-emergency-for-lgbtq-americans.

13. You can do a search for the word *justice* on a site like BibleGateway.com to get an overview; see https://www.biblegateway.com/quicksearch/?quicksearch=justice&version=NIV.

14. "How Do We Confront Our Own Blind Spots?," AskDrBrown, June 30, 2023, https://askdrbrown.org/article/how-do-we-confront-our-own-blind-spots.

15. Cindy Weinstein, ed., *The Cambridge Companion to Harriet Beecher Stowe* (New York: Cambridge University Press, 2004), 1.

16. Jonathan Kirsch, "Book Review: Provocative Call to Arms on Gay Rights," *Los Angeles Times*, October 4, 1989, https://www.latimes.com/archives/la-xpm-1989-10-04-vw-693-story.html.

17. "Gay Manifesto Outlines Game Plan for 90s," *Orlando Sentinel*, July 31, 1989, https://www.orlandosentinel.com/1989/07/31/gay-manifesto-outlines-game-plan-for-90s.

18. Kirk and Madsen, *After the Ball*.

19. Paul Bond, "Nearly 40 Percent of US Gen Zs, 30 Percent of Young Christians Identify as LGBTQ, Poll Shows," *Newsweek*, October 20, 2021, https://www.newsweek.com/nearly-40-percent-us-gen-zs-30-percent-christians-identify-lgbtq-poll-shows-1641085.

20. "The Lane Rebels and Early Anti-Slavery at Oberlin," Oberlin Sanctuary Project, accessed November 29, 2023, https://www.scalar.oberlincollegelibrary.org/sanctuary/the-lane-rebels.

21. Tim Stafford, "The Abolitionists," Christian History Institute, accessed November 29, 2023, https://christianhistoryinstitute.org/magazine/article/abolitionists.

22. Aleksandr Solzhenitsyn, "A World Split Apart," American Rhetoric, June 8, 1978, https://www.americanrhetoric.com/speeches/alexandersolzhenitsynharvard.htm.

23. Charles Colson, *God & Government: An Insider's View on the Boundaries Between Faith & Politics* (Grand Rapids: Zondervan, 2011), 378.

CHAPTER 11

1. Mike Hixenbaugh and Antonia Hylton, "Christian Activists Are Fighting to Glorify God in a Suburban Texas School District," NBC News, May 2, 2023, https://www.nbcnews.com/news/us-news/grapevine-texas-school-board-election-christian-nationalism-rcna82246.

2. Frederick Clarkson, "Dominionism-Driven Christian Nationalists for School Board," Daily Kos, December 24, 2021, https://www.dailykos.com/stories/2021/12/24/2071024/-Dominionst-Driven-Christian-Nationalists-for-School-Board.

3. Despite claims to the contrary (see Robert Farley, "Attorney General Never Called Concerned Parents 'Domestic Terrorists,'" FackCheck.org, April 22, 2022, https://www.factcheck.org/2022/04/attorney-general-never-called-concerned-parents-domestic-terrorists), this Senate interaction speaks for itself: Fred Lucas, "What This Justice Department Official Said About Treating Parents as 'Domestic Terrorists,'" Daily Signal, October 17, 2021, https://www.dailysignal.com/2021/10/07/what-this-justice-department-official-said-about-treating-parents-as-domestic-terrorists. Of course, any threats of violence or personal retaliation against school boards or school officials from aggrieved parents is completely unacceptable. That being said, this kind of over-the-top behavior does not justify equating these parents with "domestic terrorists."

4. Matt Comer, "A Prayer for Michael Brown," *QnotesCarolinas*, December 11, 2010, https://qnotescarolinas.com/a-prayer-for-michael-brown.

5. Comer, "A Prayer for Michael Brown."

6. Dr. Michael Brown, "Setting the Record Straight," *QnotesCarolinas*, December 25, 2010, https://qnotescarolinas.com/setting-the-record-straight.

7. Matt Comer, "Holy War: 'A Cause Worth Dying For,'" *QnotesCarolina*, accessed July 20, 2014, http://goqnotes.com/

editorial/editorsnote_012608.html. As of publication, the article and image were no longer available.

8. Derek Prince, *God's Word Heals* (New Kensington, PA: Whitaker House, 2010), 8.

9. Bunni Pounds, *Jesus and Politics* (Lake Mary, FL: FrontLine, 2024).

10. Dr. Michael L. Brown (@DrMichaelLBrown), "As we get closer to the frenzy and intensity of the coming election season…," X (formerly Twitter), July 19, 2023, https://twitter.com/DrMichaelLBrown/status/1681819847183806465.

11. The first part of the statement deals with allegations concerning the New Apostolic Reformation (NAR). See "NAR and Christian Nationalism Statement," NAR and Christian Nationalism, accessed February 16, 2024, https://narandchristiannationalism.com/#statement.

CHAPTER 12

1. Tom Tillison, "BlackRock CEO Talk About 'Forcing Behaviors' May Explain Why 'Woke' Runs Amok Today," American Wire News, June 5, 2023, https://americanwirenews.com/black-rock-ceo-talk-about-forcing-behaviors-may-explain-why-woke-runs-amok-today.

2. Michael Brown, "If You're Concerned About a Radical Dominionist Takeover of America Look to the Left Not the Right," The Stream, June 19, 2023, https://stream.org/if-youre-concerned-about-a-radical-dominionist-takeover-of-america-look-to-the-left-not-the-right.

3. Private email, June 20, 2023, used with permission.

4. Virginia Kruta, "James O'Keefe Drops Bombshell Video on BlackRock: 'You Got $10K? You Can Buy a Senator,'" The Daily Wire, June 20, 2023, https://www.dailywire.com/news/james-okeefe-drops-bombshell-video-on-blackrock-you-got-10k-you-can-buy-a-senator.

5. James O'Keefe (@JamesOkeefeiii), "It's not who the president is…," X (formerly Twitter), June 20, 2023, https://twitter.com/JamesOKeefeIII/status/1671262303319392259.

6. Will Hild (@WillHild), "After we exposed the ESG scam…," X (formerly Twitter), June 25, 2023, https://twitter.com/WillHild/status/1673142099150098435.

7. Spencer Brown, "BlackRock CEO Larry Fink Says He's 'Ashamed' of ESC," Townhall, June 26, 2023, https://townhall.com/tipsheet/spencerbrown/2023/06/26/larry-fink-desantis-esg-n2624984; see also Hugh Hewitt, "Jerry Bowyer: The Beginning of the End of ESG," Townhall Review With Hugh Hewitt, June 16, 2023, https://townhallreview.com/podcast/episode/8335/jerry-bowyer-the-beginning-of-the-end-of-esg.

8. John Frank, "Larry Fink 'Ashamed' to Be Part of ESG Political Debate," Axios, June 25, 2023, https://www.axios.com/2023/06/26/larry-fink-ashamed-esg-weaponized-desantis.

9. Hugh Hewitt, "Jerry Bowyer: BlackRock: Backing Off of ESG," Townhall Review With Hugh Hewitt, July 17, 2023, https://townhallreview.com/podcast/episode/8335/jerry-bowyer-blackrock-backing-off-of-esg.

10. For a five-minute animated video, see The Line of Fire, "Why Don't More Pastors Speak Out?" YouTube, November 7, 2018, https://youtu.be/gOPB2hbrqsM.

11. Brown, *A Queer Thing Happened to America*, 272–307.

12. Brown, *A Queer Thing Happened to America*, 284–285.

13. "2023 Corporate Equality Index Criteria," Human Rights Campaign, updated November 30, 2023, https://www.hrc.org/resources/corporate-equality-index-criteria.

14. "Corporate Equality Index 2023–2024," Human Rights Campaign, accessed December 1, 2023, https://www.hrc.org/resources/corporate-equality-index.

15. "Corporate Equality Index 2023-2024," Human Rights Campaign.

16. Mark Hall, "The Greatest Wealth Transfer in History: What's Happening and What Are the Implications," *Forbes*, November 11, 2019, https://www.forbes.com/sites/markhall/2019/11/11/the-greatest-wealth-transfer-in-history-whats-happening-and-what-are-the-implications/?sh=3a0eb9f64090.

CHAPTER 13

1. John Wesley, "Do all the good you can...," BrainyQuote, accessed December 1, 2023, https://www.brainyquote.com/quotes/john_wesley_524889.

2. D. L. Moody, *One Thousand and One Thoughts From My Library* (New York: Fleming H. Revell, 1898), 130.

3. "Who Are the Islamic 'Morality Police'?," BBC News, April 22, 2016, https://www.bbc.com/news/world-middle-east-36101150.

4. William Booth, "Go straight for souls...," BrainyQuote, accessed December 1, 2023, https://www.brainyquote.com/quotes/william_booth_380954.

5. "Charles Spurgeon Quotes on Evangelism," Coming in the Clouds, February 3, 2020, https://comingintheclouds.org/christian-resources/evangelism/charles-spurgeon-quotes-on-evangelism.

6. See Justin Brierly, *Unbelievable? Why After Ten Years of Talking With Atheists, I'm Still a Christian* (London: SPCK, 2017).

7. Tom Skinner, *How Black Is the Gospel* (Philadelphia: Lippincott, 1970), 5.